WINGS TO FLY

Kaamendra Dahat

ISBN 979-8-89322-860-1

I dedicate this book to my wife, Paurnima, whose unwavering support has been the foundation of my journey studying abroad. I also wish to extend my heartfelt thanks to all those who have supported me from my days as a teacher to my current role as the Founder-CEO of three companies.

I am thankful to the parents and students who have placed their trust in me, inspiring me to continually push forward. I am also grateful to the educational institutions, trustees, principals, and faculties who have welcomed me to deliver seminars, providing valuable insights on educational and career opportunities abroad. Your support has helped thousands of students pave their path to success overseas.

Kaamendra Dahat

CONTENTS

ABOUT THE BOOK

In this increasingly interconnected world, the pursuit of education transcends borders, offering students unparalleled opportunities for personal, academic, and professional growth. Whether driven by a desire for cultural immersion, access to specialized programs, or exposure to diverse perspectives, seeking education on an international scale has become a compelling endeavor for individuals worldwide.

In this rapidly changing scenario of global education, navigating the various options and complexities can be daunting. From choosing the right destination and institution to understanding visa requirements and cultural nuances, embarking on an international educational journey requires careful planning and informed decision-making.

This book serves as a beacon for those embarking on this transformative path, offering invaluable insights, practical advice, and expert guidance to navigate the labyrinth of international education. Whether you are a high school student exploring study abroad opportunities, a graduate student seeking advanced degrees in a foreign land, or a professional looking to enhance your skills through international programs, this book is your comprehensive companion.

Drawing upon the collective wisdom of educators, counselors, and seasoned travelers, we delve into the essential aspects of international education. From selecting the right program and financing your studies to adapting to a new cultural milieu and leveraging global networks, each chapter is meticulously crafted to address the multifaceted dimensions of studying abroad.

Through real-life anecdotes, expert insights, and actionable tips, we aim to empower you to make informed decisions and embark on a fulfilling educational journey that transcends borders. This book will equip you with the knowledge and confidence to turn your international education dreams into reality.

As you turn the pages of this book, may you find inspiration, clarity, and the courage to embrace the enriching opportunities that await you on your global educational odyssey. Welcome aboard as we embark together on this transformative quest for knowledge, growth, and cultural understanding.

ABOUT THE AUTHOR

After completing my education and getting few years work experience as a teacher in India, I went to England to pursue an MBA from London, United Kingdom. Over the years, I have been instrumental in assisting more than 6000 students in their educational journeys, directing them towards choosing guided careers, and the success rate of the student placement is 100%. I bring 18 years of dedicated experience in the field of International Education.

As the CEO of Interedwise Education Pvt. Ltd., I am instrumental in:

- Consistently maintaining a high level of professionalism and service.

- University and associate relationships.

- I have conducted about 1000 career guidance seminars for various levels of students.

- Overall development of the company.

- Delivered more than 3000 hours of career guidance seminars for different levels of Indian students.

- Overlooking the team to develop and implement a number of marketing initiatives. Supervising and motivating my team and franchise partners.

Awards and Recognition:

- Awarded the 'Partner Of The Year Award' by the British Council.

- Received 'The Maharashtra Ratna Award 2023'.

- Recognized with 'The Global Service Company of the Year' at the Vyaapar Jagat Awards 2021.

- Honored with the 'Indian Achievers Award' for outstanding achievement in Education and Social Service.

- Holds ICEF AGENCY STATUS - ACCREDITED #5381.

- Certified as an ICEF Trained Agent Counsellor - ITAC#1938.

- Graduate of the Canada Course – Education Agent – CCG#2020.

- Completed "Building Effective Professional Networks And Relationships" course by **Central Queensland University, Australia**.

- Earned the UK Agent and Counsellor Training Certification Award from the British Council – Certificate Code #1541.

- Received the Irish Education Graduate Award #185.

- Completed "Entrepreneurship: From Business Idea To Action" a course by **Kings College, London**.

- Awarded a Certificate of Appreciation by **Dr. D Y Patil College of Pharmacy.**

INDEX

- Parents visit

- Spouse/Child/Parent dependent visa

- Part-time jobs

- Rules

- Work culture

- Get together with industry specialists, experts

Availability of financial aid, scholarship, bursary, educational loans available

- Finance - scholarship, bursary

- Education loan and recommendation

Rules and Regulations

- Pre-departure briefing and creating awareness- Instructions for students.

- Rules and Regulations

- Registering with local GP (Physician)

- Insurance international (Importance of Insurance)

- Discount Student Card/SIM Card/Bank Account in Overseas Banks

- Work during studies.

- List of Clothing – Do we need to put this? (Things to carry to different countries)

- Privacy Policy

- Awareness about other cases

- Working Culture - Respect for each person/job, No work pressure, Good Working environment, Weekly payment schedule, Importance of privacy at work and home.

Value of Degree

Post Study Visa

- Immigration Rules

- Visa transfer - Switching of Visa from student to work

- Post study Visa

  Free Education

  Time Management

- How to classify work-Urgent vs important

- Adjusting time between job and academics

Progress in comfort zone

Taxation

- Awareness of taxation and finding a realistic earning package.

- Salary vs Tax

- Living Cost

Overseas Education- Going without support and guidance

- Hidden costs of studying abroad

- Lack of assessment/guidance

- Pros and Cons of Studying Abroad

- Confusion in counsellors

- The Significance of Setting Clear Goals and Objectives for Students

- How your personality can drive your career decision.

- Promising countries for international Education

- Emerging Trends/Courses

- Coming back and creating job opportunities in India

THE LURE OF STUDYING OVERSEAS

Instances have surfaced where certain students exhibit limited interest in pursuing education but are more enticed by the prospect of relocating overseas for the lifestyle it promises. Unfortunately, some of these individuals aim to bypass essential steps, such as undertaking elementary English aptitude tests and meeting mandatory requirements. In their pursuit, they often opt for dubious colleges, leading to frequent refusals. In rare instances where admissions are secured, subsequent discoveries reveal that these colleges operate improperly and are eventually shut down. As a consequence, these students find themselves compelled to return to India.

Certain consultants, driven by a desire for quick financial gains, may engage in facilitating admissions to such unreliable institutions, neglecting the potential consequences. This unethical practice not only tarnishes the reputation of the consultants involved, but also casts a shadow on the entire education industry. The most egregious outcome of these actions is jeopardizing students' careers, highlighting the urgent need for ethical conduct and transparency in the education consulting sector.

Geographical preferences have significantly influenced migration decisions. For instance, there has been a mass migration of Punjabis to Canada, while students from Andhra and Tamil Nadu often choose the United States. Large numbers of Gujaratis have opted for the UK or the US, and Keralites have predominantly selected Arab countries, primarily for job opportunities rather than education.

In the early post-independence decades, from 1947 until the 1970s, the phenomenon of Brain Drain was primarily observed among the talented and privileged class. Individuals from this group, including prominent industrialists such as Ratan Tata, Rahul Bajaj, Baba Kalyani, Azim Premji, and others, pursued education abroad, often through self-funding or scholarships. Notably, many of them returned to India after their studies. However, the trend during this period saw a significant number of individuals choosing to settle abroad, mainly due to limited job opportunities in India.

From the 1980s to the late 1990s, there was a notable surge in the number of Indians relocating abroad. This trend was primarily fueled by the economic challenges faced by India, worsened by the decade-long License Raj Policy. Additionally, the IT sector experienced a significant boom in Western countries, particularly Silicon Valley, attracting young engineers. This period saw the migration of notable figures like Sundar Pichai, Satya Nadella, and other Indian American CEOs.

The 1980s and late 1990s proved to be an opportune time for individuals to migrate and settle in the US, UK, and European countries. The global landscape had opened up with the fall of the Soviet Union, ushering in the era of globalization. These countries actively welcomed immigrants, making it an advantageous period for those who seized the opportunity.

The third migration phase, from the 2000s to the 2010s, was marked by a significant increase in the number of people moving abroad. This surge can be attributed to the onsite opportunities provided by IT companies, the growing interest in pursuing MS/MBA degrees due to readily available bank loans, and the aspiration of those who couldn't migrate during the earlier phases to ensure that their children or relatives could move abroad. Various factors, including the pursuit of quality education and better salaries, motivated individuals during this period. This trend persisted despite challenges such as the 9/11 attacks and the global impact of the Covid-19 pandemic.

Punjab and International Migration

In few North Indian states, the fervor among students to pursue higher education abroad and ultimately settle there persists relentlessly. The enthusiasm is so intense that parents, despite facing financial constraints, spare no effort to turn their children's aspirations into reality. Struggling financially, parents go to great lengths to support their children's dreams, securing loans from banks, mortgaging their homes and land, and borrowing money from relatives, even if it means plunging into significant debt.

Reports from Punjab suggest an alarming scenario where entire villages are becoming deserted, and people are resorting to selling their lands. This trend implies that those leaving the state have no intention of returning. Beyond the scarcity of job opportunities within the state, students in Punjab seem to be grappling with the challenge of accessing quality education. Experts argue that unless systemic issues in Punjab are addressed, this ongoing exodus could compound the challenges faced by the state.

The rush among Punjab youngsters for IELTS and migration can be attributed to the allure of the Canadian and American Dream, influenced by those who have already established themselves abroad. This trend has become a chain reaction, fueled by individuals settled in Canada showcasing a glamorous and comfortable lifestyle.

A Desire to Immigrate to Canada

Here's a case of a Maharashtrian doctor from Mumbai with a Punjabi wife. They came to me with a desire to immigrate to Canada, seeing the common trend of Punjabis moving to Canada. When I reviewed their profile, I questioned the doctor about his decision, noting that he already had a successful practice in Maharashtra. His response emphasized his desire to provide his child with a high-quality education and lifestyle, which he believed might be challenging to achieve in India.

Considering various immigration factors, I suggested that Canada might not be the most suitable option. Instead, I recommended New Zealand as a more fitting destination. Both the doctor and his wife were convinced by my reasoning, leading them to choose New Zealand for their relocation. The doctor has successfully immigrated on a study visa to New Zealand and now, post-completion of education, is serving in the Public Health Services in New Zealand.

Numerous individuals aspire to attain permanent residency in Canada. Several agencies operate on the premise of securing payment upfront, offering enticing assurances of facilitating this permanent residency. However, there is often a lack of clarity and certainty in the process, with the entire procedure potentially spanning 1 to 3 years in terms of processing time.

A Bank Manager's Unsuccessful Attempts To Immigrate To Canada

Another case is of a bank manager from Mumbai with 8-9 years of experience who approached me with the aspiration of immigrating to Canada. I had previously assisted his nephew in pursuing a course in Canada that ultimately led to obtaining permanent residency (PR). The bank manager shared his frustration about unsuccessful attempts over the past 3-4 years with various consultants. After conducting a thorough assessment, I conveyed the reality of his situation, highlighting that his age - 38 then - would not help him secure any points for PR, a crucial detail none of the previous consultants had disclosed.

Six months later, he returned, inquiring about the possibility of obtaining a letter from a university and a visa to study in Canada. Agreeing to take on this new challenge, I processed his application, securing an offer letter from a Canadian University and swiftly processing his visa. Now, he resides in Canada with his family, having completed his education there. With a three-year post-study visa following two years of education, he currently holds a promising banking job in Canada. As he progresses in his career, he is well on his way to securing permanent residency (PR). Once you have Canadian experience and education, it is easy to get PR . So, although a long process, he was able to fulfill his requirement.

Informed Guidance

In another case, a family of doctors sought my assistance for their daughter's education. Initially, she chose Switzerland but returned after a year, dissatisfied. Upon her request for another country, I recommended New Zealand, where she was satisfied in her course and studies.

Later, the couple approached me again, this time for their son. They revealed that he had refrained from attending school since 11th grade due to a false accusation by a teacher, causing humiliation in front of the class. After meeting the son, who displayed brilliance, I learned about his disinterest in Indian institutes. We evaluated his 10th credentials and tried applying on this basis, but it did not work. I then asked him to get his 11th-grade result. With an additional year of experience, I processed his application to a UK institute based on these documents. He excelled in the IELTS exam, completing his Higher National Certificate (HNC) & Higher National Diploma (HND) in two years, followed by a third-year mechanical degree.

Upon returning to India for a job, he faced saturation in the job market. Seeking guidance again, I recommended pursuing a postgraduation in Canada. Successfully completing his postgraduation, he secured a rewarding job in Canada.

This case underscores how timely and informed guidance can shape a student's bright career path.

THE DRIVING FACTORS FOR STUDYING ABROAD

The pursuit of higher education presents a myriad of opportunities and challenges for students globally. Many are drawn to the idea of studying abroad, seeking new experiences and academic advancements in different cultural and educational settings. There are several key reasons why students opt for higher education abroad, with varying levels of certainty about their plans. Around 60% of students are eager to secure employment in their host country upon completing their studies, often with the intent of extending their stay. They are motivated by better career prospects, exposure to a new professional environment, and the opportunity to build a network in the country of study. The allure of gaining international work experience and cultural immersion is a significant driving force for many.

Conversely, approximately 20% of students may embark on their educational journey abroad without a clearly defined purpose or plan. Their decision may be influenced by advice from alumni, friends, relatives, or parents. While this presents an exciting opportunity, it's crucial for these students to critically evaluate their motivations and expectations before committing. Considering the potential impact on their future career path and personal growth is essential.

The remaining 20% of students demonstrate a high level of certainty about studying abroad. Their motivations often center around pursuing a specific course from a particular educational institution, driven by the desire to access specialized expertise, advanced research facilities, or renowned faculty members. These students typically have a clear vision of their academic and professional goals and are dedicated to achieving them through international education.

For students, whether uncertain or resolute in their plans to study abroad, thorough research and due diligence are paramount. It's essential to gather comprehensive information about the destination country and potential institutions, including the socio-political climate, immigration policies, and other factors that could impact educational and career pursuits. Understanding potential challenges and opportunities enables students to make informed decisions and navigate their academic journey confidently.

The decision to pursue higher education abroad is deeply personal and multi-faceted for each student. Whether driven by career aspirations, external influences, or educational objectives, it's crucial for students to approach their international academic pursuits with careful consideration and preparation. By acknowledging the diverse motivations and uncertainties students may encounter.

MOTIVATION TO STUDY ABROAD

Why are Parents and Students Motivated to Study Abroad?

The limited capacity of Indian universities to accommodate the growing number of students has created a pressing need for additional educational institutions. This scarcity is a significant factor driving Indian students to pursue education abroad. Furthermore, the allure of American and European lifestyles, along with the advanced infrastructure in these regions, has been a longstanding influence.

Compounding this, the substantial income disparity between India and these foreign countries is a compelling motivator. The remuneration for similar job roles abroad is nearly ten times higher than what is offered in India. Despite the higher cost of living overseas, when converted to Indian currency, the earning potential becomes exceptionally lucrative—often ranging from 80 to 100 times more than what is available domestically. It is this definite contrast in economic opportunities that prompts many students to choose international education with the prospect of settling in these developed nations.

Furthermore, individuals working abroad have the convenience of accessing luxury with a simple click, contributing to an overall improved lifestyle. Many Indians are drawn to studying abroad due to the enhanced research opportunities and the comparatively limited avenues for research in India. Headlines frequently feature Indian-origin scientists making groundbreaking discoveries, and some have even been honored with Nobel Prizes in the field of research and development. This success is attributed to the robust support systems, advanced infrastructure, facilities, and expansive opportunities available abroad.

Parents are increasingly inclined to provide their children with diverse exposures, particularly as graduates from engineering and pharmaceutical colleges often face a scarcity of local job opportunities. The willingness to send their children overseas is fueled by the open immigration policies of foreign governments, the shortage of occupations, and the multitude of opportunities presented in various fields.

- Facilities in Foreign Universities

- Infrastructure

- Higher Salaries

- Better Standard of Living

- Enhanced opportunities

INFLUENCE OF ALUMNI, RELATIVES, FRIENDS, AND FAMILY

The Parents' Concerns

Parents often have legitimate concerns when considering sending their children for overseas education. These concerns typically revolve around various aspects of the academic, social, and personal well-being of their children. I've encountered two distinct types of parents:

1. North Indians:

– Their primary concern revolves around a straightforward question - "Can we secure a visa?" That's the extent of their focus. For them, the service is predominantly required up to the visa stage.

2. West Indians:

– In contrast, West Indian parents express a different set of concerns. They inquire about lifestyle, accommodation options, types of food available, weather conditions, and potential challenges like racism. Unlike North Indian parents, West Indian parents often assume that arranging admission and securing a visa can be managed, but they seek more comprehensive information about living standards. In these cases, a significant amount of persuasion and clarification is necessary to make them aware of the various aspects and possibilities beyond just admission and visa processing.

Deciding to pursue studies abroad holds the potential to profoundly shape a student's life. It provides exposure to diverse cultures, languages, and academic environments. However, this choice can be influenced by the expectations and pressures exerted by parents, alumni, and relatives.

Parental expectations and pressure exert a significant influence on a student's decision to study abroad. Often, parents draw from their own experiences and beliefs regarding the value of international education. Positive experiences or success stories from family members or acquaintances who studied abroad may encourage parents to advocate for a similar path for their child. Conversely, negative experiences or misconceptions may lead parents to express reservations or dissuade their child from pursuing studies abroad.

Alumni who have previously studied abroad can also wield considerable influence. Their first-hand experiences and achievements serve as compelling motivators for current students considering similar opportunities. Alumni may offer invaluable guidance, insights, and personal anecdotes that shape a student's perception of the benefits of studying abroad.

Additionally, the influence of relatives, such as older siblings or cousins, cannot be overlooked. Their experiences or advice may sway a student's perspective on studying abroad, either positively or negatively.

Moreover, parental expectations and pressure may stem from cultural norms, societal expectations, and financial considerations. In certain cultures, studying abroad is esteemed as a prestigious opportunity and a gateway to enhanced career prospects. Consequently, parents may exert greater pressure on their children to pursue international education, driven by aspirations for their child's success.

Financial concerns further intensify parental expectations and pressure. The substantial costs associated with studying abroad, encompassing tuition fees, living expenses, and travel expenses, may prompt parents to set specific expectations regarding their child's academic performance, choice of institution, and field of study.

Despite these influences, it is imperative for students to navigate the decision-making process with clear communication and a steadfast understanding of their personal aspirations and goals. Open dialogue with parents, alumni, and relatives can provide students with a comprehensive understanding of studying abroad and facilitate the addressing of any concerns or misconceptions.

While parental expectations and pressure hold sway, it is essential for students to make well-informed decisions aligned with their individual aspirations, academic interests, and long-term career objectives. By seeking counsel from diverse sources and maintaining open communication, students can confidently embark on the opportunities presented by studying abroad while also navigating parental, alumni, and familial expectations and pressures.

HOW TO CHOOSE YOUR STUDY ABROAD DESTINATION?

Country and Courses

Certain countries are renowned for their expertise in specific industries, offering robust courses tailored to prepare students for careers in those fields.

For example, individuals interested in pursuing a major in Computer Science and a minor in Music may find an abundance of specialized programs in the USA, along with numerous universities offering comprehensive coursework in this area. The UK is another country known for its strong offerings in multiple domains.

Similarly, disciplines such as Interior Fashion Design or Management are often associated with countries like Italy, Sweden, or France, where institutions offer top-notch programs designed to equip students with the skills needed for success in these industries. Switzerland, recognized as the birthplace of Hospitality, is a popular destination for those interested in Hotel Management due to its renowned educational facilities and industry connections.

Ultimately, the choice of country and institution depends on the specific course of study and the facilities available during and after completion of the program.

CULTURAL DIFFERENCES

Establishing international connections and networks holds significant advantages for students intending to pursue studies abroad in countries like the UK, USA, Ireland, Canada, Australia, New Zealand, and EU nations. These connections serve as valuable assets, providing support and opening doors to opportunities both during their time abroad and in their future careers.

Primarily, international connections broaden students' perspectives and deepen their understanding of diverse cultures, traditions, and perspectives. Engaging with peers from various backgrounds fosters a global mindset and enhances cultural competency, essential qualities for thriving in an interconnected world where cross-cultural interactions are vital.

Furthermore, an international network offers practical benefits for students navigating life abroad. From sharing insights on local academic systems to offering tips on accommodation and visa procedures, these connections facilitate a smoother transition into the foreign educational environment, making the experience more enriching and enjoyable.

In terms of career prospects, international connections can be transformative. They provide access to internships, job placements, and collaborative projects, while also serving as a source of mentorship and career guidance. In today's global job market, candidates with international experiences and a diverse network are highly sought after, as they demonstrate adaptability and cross-cultural communication skills essential for success in diverse professional settings.

Ultimately, fostering international connections enriches students' academic journeys and positions them for success in their future careers. Encouraging students to embrace opportunities to connect with peers worldwide not only enhances their educational experience but also equips them with the tools needed to make a meaningful impact on a global scale.

AWARENESS ABOUT CLIMATE AND PRECAUTIONS

Raising awareness about climate and taking precautions before embarking on a study abroad program can significantly enhance students' experiences in a responsible and seamless manner. Here are some essential points for students to consider:

1. Understanding Weather Patterns: Conduct thorough research on the typical climate and weather conditions of your chosen study abroad destination. This would enable you to pack appropriate clothing and prepare for any weather-related circumstances you may encounter.

2. Environmental Consciousness: Practice awareness regarding the environmental impact of various activities and behaviors. By adopting sustainable practices, such as utilizing public transportation and minimizing plastic consumption, you can positively influence the local environment.

3. Health Precautions: Be aware of the potential health risks associated with climate-related factors in specific regions, such as high altitudes, extreme temperatures, or allergens. This may involve taking necessary vaccinations and health safety measures.

4. Preparedness for Natural Disasters: Be informed about the likelihood of natural disasters in certain areas and read on evacuation protocols, emergency procedures, and communication channels in the event of such occurrences.

5. Cultural Sensitivity: Explore the cultural significance of climate-related elements in the destination country. This includes understanding how weather influences local customs, traditions, and ways of life, fostering a deeper appreciation for diverse cultures.

6. Responsible Resource Management: Promote responsible resource utilization by being aware of energy conservation, water consumption, and waste management practices in the host country.

7. Adaptation Strategies: Help develop adaptive strategies for adjusting to climate differences, whether it involves acclimating to a new climate or mitigating the impact of weather-related challenges on daily routines.

By integrating these considerations into their pre-departure preparations, students can cultivate a global perspective, demonstrate respect for local ecosystems, and make positive contributions to the communities they will be visiting.

SOCIAL ACTIVITIES

Managing the intricacies of social interactions and cultural disparities while raising a child together in a foreign country can be a daunting yet enlightening journey for separated parents. In such circumstances, parents not only grapple with the responsibilities of co-parenting but also confront the complexities of assimilating into a new cultural milieu.

One significant hurdle they may face pertains to the divergence in societal norms concerning adolescent social engagements. Across various countries, parents often hold contrasting viewpoints regarding granting independence to their teenage children, particularly those aged 14 and above, to venture out at night. This can precipitate conflicts and discord as parents strive to balance their child's desire for autonomy with the imperative of setting reasonable boundaries. Navigating these disparities in cultural norms necessitates a learning ground for both parents to find common ground that respects each other's values while acknowledging the nuances of the new cultural context.

Furthermore, disparities in perceptions of etiquette and propriety can vary markedly between cultures. Conduct deemed courteous and respectful in one country may be construed as inappropriate or disrespectful in another. Parents may find themselves grappling with these disparities not only in their own conduct but also in guiding their child to comprehend and adapt to the cultural intricacies of their new surroundings. Negotiating this terrain requires open communication, flexibility, and mutual respect.

However, amidst these challenges lies the opportunity to project a positive image of a student's home country by upholding cherished values and making constructive contributions to the host society. By demonstrating reverence for local customs, actively engaging in community endeavors, and embracing cultural idiosyncrasies, students can foster understanding and goodwill, potentially building a favorable perception of their homeland among the local populace.

The experience of separated parents raising their child together in a foreign land presents a blend of hurdles and triumphs. It demands empathy, adaptability, and a willingness to find common ground amid cultural dissonance. Successfully surmounting these challenges can not only fortify the bond between the parents but also offer a rewarding experience for their child, providing a platform to positively showcase the values of their home country on the global stage.

AWARENESS OF TAXATION LAWS

Understanding taxation and accurately calculating potential earnings while considering living expenses and savings after deductions are crucial steps for students and professionals contemplating a move to a different country. Whether the relocation is for academic pursuits, career opportunities, or personal reasons, having a grasp of taxation and living costs in the destination nation is vital for effective financial planning and decision-making.

Initially, it's imperative that you familiarize yourself with the tax system of the intended country of relocation. Each country has its own tax laws, rates, and structures, which can significantly impact the net income one receives. Consulting financial experts or utilizing country-specific resources can aid in comprehending the portion of income that will be allocated towards taxes.

Subsequently, it is essential to compute a realistic earning package. This process involves assessing gross income, incorporating taxes, and then determining net income. Moreover, it is crucial to factor in living expenses such as accommodation, utilities, transportation, groceries, healthcare, and other necessities particular to the destination country. Additionally, accounting for unforeseen expenses or fluctuations in currency exchange rates can enhance the accuracy of the calculation.

Once taxes and expenses have been deducted from your gross income, you can evaluate the amount that can realistically be saved or allocated towards other financial objectives. This step provides a clearer understanding of the actual financial advantages of relocating to a new country.

If you are comprehending the financial implications of studying abroad, considering living expenses and taxes is essential for effective budgeting and financial planning. Exploring part-time job opportunities and potential scholarships can also aid in managing expenses.

If you are contemplating a job relocation, you should thoroughly analyze the overall compensation package, including benefits, bonuses, and allowances, in addition to taxation and living expenses. Adopting this holistic approach can offer a more comprehensive understanding of the financial ramifications of the relocation.

Furthermore, it is crucial to be aware of any tax treaties or agreements between one's home country and the destination country, as these can influence how income is taxed and impact overall financial circumstances.

Being mindful of taxation and calculating a realistic earning package that considers living costs and savings after deductions is imperative for anyone contemplating a move abroad. Through diligent research, seeking advice, and considering all financial aspects, students and professionals can make well-informed decisions regarding their international pursuits and ensure enhanced financial stability in the long term.

EDUCATIONAL SYSTEMS: INDIA VS EUROPE

There are certain distinctive features that set apart the educational systems of India and Europe. Despite both systems aiming to foster academic excellence and personal development, significant differences emerge in their structures, approaches, and cultural contexts.

1. Structural Variances

– Indian Education System: Adheres to a 10+2+3 structure, comprising 10 years of primary and secondary education, followed by 2 years of higher secondary education and 3 years of undergraduate studies with additional years of studies for bachelor's degrees in engineering, Medicine, Dentistry, Veterinary science, Law, Architecture, etc. One has to spend a minimum of 3 more years to get a doctorate in the particular subject area. Indian students can complete their diplomas in a particular subject area after 10+2, and the duration of the diploma varies from 2 to 3 years.

– European Education System: Follows a 10+2+4 structure, with 3 to 4 years dedicated to undergraduate studies, which may include a placement (Internship) year, 2 years for master's studies, and 3 to 4 years for doctoral studies. Bachelor's degrees in medicine, dentistry, veterinary science, and law, with a few more years of study. One has to spend a minimum of 4 years to complete a doctorate in a particular subject area. European students can go for specialized studies of a 2-year bachelor's degree, known as an associate degree. After completing an associate degree, one can go for employment, but one cannot get admission for a master's degree unless one has completed a bachelor's degree.

2. Specialization Dynamics

– India: Students typically choose their specialization after completing higher secondary education, opting for streams like science, commerce, or arts.

– Europe: Offers greater flexibility, allowing students to select their area of specialization during undergraduate or graduate studies.

3. Assessment Approaches

– Indian System: Heavily reliant on examinations, emphasizing memorization and rote learning.

– European System: Balances coursework, assignments, projects, and examinations, promoting critical thinking and practical application of knowledge.

4. Focus on Vocational Training

– India: Gradually integrating vocational training but with a stronger emphasis on academic education.

– Europe: Emphasizes vocational and technical training, equipping students with practical skills aligned with specific industries.

5. Affordability and Accessibility

– India: This can be financially burdensome for many students and families, hindering accessibility for certain socio-economic groups.

- Europe: Generally, offers more affordable or subsidized education, with low or no tuition fees in many cases.

6. Research Emphasis

- India: Research opportunities exist but are not as widespread across the education system.

- Europe: Prioritizes research and innovation, providing extensive opportunities and facilities for students.

7. Cultural and Regional Diversity

- India: Reflects diverse cultural, regional, and linguistic backgrounds, contributing to the richness of its educational landscape.

- Europe: Exhibits diversity, albeit often on a smaller scale compared to India's vast cultural and linguistic variations.

These comparisons show how education in India and Europe differs. It's important to understand and adjust to these differences when studying in different places.

EDUCATIONAL SYSTEMS: INDIA VS THE US

The key distinctions between the educational systems of India and the United States, highlight how students experience schooling differently in each country.

1. Structure and Duration

– India: The system spans 10+2 years, consisting of 10 years of primary and secondary education followed by 2 years of higher secondary education.

– US: Students complete 12 years of schooling, divided into elementary (grades 1-5), middle (grades 6-8), and high school (grades 9-12).

2. Specialization

– India: Specialization typically occurs after 10th grade, with students choosing between sciences, commerce, or arts (humanities).

– US: Students benefit from a more flexible curriculum, allowing exploration before choosing a specialization in college.

3. Standardized Tests

– India: Board exams like State Boards, CBSE or ICSE are pivotal for student evaluation.

– US: Standardized tests such as the SAT or ACT are common for college admissions but aren't the sole determining factor.

4. Teaching Methods

– India: Emphasizes rote learning and textbook knowledge, often teacher-centric.

– US: Focuses on interactive, participatory methods to encourage critical thinking and independent research.

5. Cost

– India: Public schools offer subsidized education, while private schools tend to be pricier.

– US: Public schools are funded by taxpayers and generally free for residents, with private schools requiring tuition fees.

6. Higher Education

– India: Universities and colleges provide undergraduate and postgraduate degrees.

– US: Offers a diverse range of higher education institutions, including universities, Institutes of Technologies, and community colleges, granting bachelor's, master's, and doctoral degrees.

These comparisons shed light on the diverse approaches to education in India and the US. While each system has its strengths and weaknesses, understanding these differences is crucial for students navigating their educational journeys.

TYPES OF UNIVERSITIES

It is imperative to recognize the conventional emphasis placed on university rankings within traditional systems. There is often a strong inclination towards pursuing admission at top-ranking educational institutions, a sentiment widely shared among students. However, this singular focus on rankings may inadvertently overshadow the significance of course content.

It is crucial for students to consider the merit of course content and employability prospects offered by medium-ranking universities. In instances where a medium-ranking university boasts exemplary course offerings and favorable employability outcomes, serious consideration should be given.

Ivy League Institutions

For those inclined towards research-oriented pursuits, top-ranking universities typically offer an array of resources, including extensive research facilities, participation in public actions, international conferences, and robust industry partnerships. Such institutions are often ideal for individuals seeking research-based programs.

While prestigious groups such as the Ivy League or Group of Eight universities, Russell group universities boast exceptional rankings, it is essential to acknowledge their typically private/public nature, resulting in higher costs that may be prohibitive for many students. While scholarships may be available, they are often limited for international students and may not cover a substantial portion of tuition fees. Therefore, students should be realistic in their expectations, understanding that significant scholarships, ranging from 70% to 100%, are rarely feasible.

Applied/Millennium Group Universities

Alternatively, for students primarily concerned with securing employment post-graduation, factors such as alumni employability, career prospects, university location, and affordability of tuition and living expenses are of paramount importance. These variables are contingent upon both the location and ranking of the university.

Consideration of industrial tie-ups, internship opportunities, and the potential for exchange programs with other universities further enriches the educational experience and enhances exposure for students.

Exceptional opportunities for students to acquire valuable work experience and industry connections abound, particularly in institutions with strong ties to various industries.

In Ireland, the Institute of Technology stands out as a prime example. These institutes specialize in STEM programs and offer curricula meticulously crafted in collaboration with industry professionals. This unique approach ensures that graduates are well-prepared to excel in their respective fields upon entering the workforce, making it an attractive option for students aspiring to secure lucrative employment opportunities.

Course-Specific Group of Institutes

Furthermore, students seeking specialized education in specific disciplines, such as creative arts, may find that course-specific institutes cater precisely to their needs. While these institutions may not boast top rankings, their focused expertise in particular subjects renders them invaluable for individuals aiming to hone their skills and pursue careers in niche industries.

Difference Between STEM/NON-STEM

STEM programs are highly sought after in many countries, with STEM standing for Science, Technology, Engineering, and Mathematics. Graduates from these programs often receive priority for job opportunities and are encouraged to stay in countries such as the USA, UK, Canada, Australia, New Zealand, Germany, France, Finland, and Denmark.

In the United States, for instance, students enrolled in STEM programs are granted extended stay duration compared to those in non-STEM programs. Consequently, individuals pursuing non-STEM programs may encounter challenges in settling in these countries. Hence, it is imperative for students opting for non-STEM programs to thoroughly research the options for staying back and job prospects in their destination country. Seeking guidance from experts is advisable to gain insights into the prevailing market conditions.

Moreover, it's essential to note that true mastery of a subject often requires practical work experience in addition to academic study.

SCHOLARSHIPS

Scholarships can serve as a crucial support system for students seeking education abroad. Whether aiming for study destinations like the United States, the United Kingdom, Australia, Canada, or elsewhere, Indian students have access to a multitude of scholarships. These opportunities ease financial constraints and pave the way for realizing their aspirations of international education.

Institutional Scholarships:

Numerous universities and colleges worldwide extend scholarships to international students, including those hailing from India. These scholarships may hinge on academic achievements, financial requirements, specialized fields of study, or a blend of criteria. Among the institutions recognized for their generous scholarship provisions for Indian students are:

1. Fulbright Scholarships: Funded by the U.S. government, Fulbright scholarships aid students pursuing master's or Ph.D. degrees at universities in the United States.

2. Chevening Scholarships: Supported by the British government, Chevening Scholarships assist students pursuing postgraduate degrees in the United Kingdom.

3. Australia Awards: Offered by the Australian government, these scholarships cater to Indian students across all academic levels, ranging from undergraduate to postdoctoral research.

Indian Government Scholarships:

The Indian government also extends numerous scholarships for students aspiring to study abroad. Among these, some well-known options include:

1. Scholarship for Higher Education (SHE): Provided by the Department of Science and Technology, this scholarship aids outstanding students in pursuing advanced studies in basic and natural sciences.

2. Commonwealth Scholarship and Fellowship Plan: Managed by the Ministry of Education, this scholarship assists Indian students in pursuing master's and Ph.D. programs in the United Kingdom.

Foreign Government Scholarships:

Several foreign governments extend scholarships to international students, including those from India. Highlighted programs include:

1. Erasmus Mundus Scholarships: Backed by the European Union, these scholarships allow students worldwide to pursue studies across Europe.

2. New Zealand Scholarships: Provided by the New Zealand government, these scholarships cater to Indian students seeking undergraduate and postgraduate education in New Zealand.

Organizational Scholarships:

Numerous organizations, both in India and overseas, extend scholarships to Indian students pursuing education abroad. Some prominent examples include:

1. Tata Scholarships for Cornell University: This scholarship assists Indian students applying for undergraduate studies at Cornell University.

2. Rotary Foundation Global Grant: Rotary International provides scholarships to aid graduate-level academic pursuits in fields relevant to Rotary's humanitarian efforts.

Eligibility Criteria for These Scholarships:

The eligibility criteria for each scholarship differ, but typical requirements may encompass:

1. Academic Achievement: The majority of scholarships necessitate a robust academic background along with standardized test scores such as the GRE, GMAT, or IELTS.

2. Financial Assistance: Certain scholarships are awarded based on financial need, requiring applicants to demonstrate their financial circumstances.

3. Personal Statement: Many scholarships mandate a compelling essay delineating academic objectives, career aspirations, and motivations for application.

4. Recommendation Letters: Applicants may be required to furnish letters of recommendation from professors, employers, or other professionals who can vouch for their capabilities.

5. Interview: Some scholarships may entail an interview as part of the selection process.

It is crucial when seeking scholarships to thoroughly examine the eligibility criteria, application deadlines, and necessary documentation for each opportunity. Through dedicated research and application efforts, Indian students can effectively diminish financial obstacles to studying abroad and unlock access to top-tier education. Keep in mind that every scholarship presents distinct prerequisites and timelines. Thus, it's advisable to plan meticulously and submit applications well ahead of deadlines to enhance the likelihood of obtaining financial support for overseas studies.

VALUE OF DEGREE (STUDY VS EMPLOYABILITY)

This is a very important aspect of shortlisting a degree, institute, and country because much depends on the applicability of the degree in your home country. If you wish to come back and practice in your home country, you have to ensure some things before investing your time and money.

If the degree pursued by a student abroad is not recognized in India, obtaining a visa becomes challenging. For instance, to become a teacher in the UK, one must enroll in the PGCE (Post Graduate Certificate in Education). However, this particular degree is not offered to international students. Opting for such a program may prompt immigration officers to question the choice, as it is not valid in the student's home country. In India, a B.Ed. is a valid and mandatory degree considered for teaching.

For those aspiring to teach in the UK, my recommendation is to pursue an M.A. in Education first. Upon completion, securing a post-study visa allows for employment, and concurrently, one can pursue the PGCE. Opting for a non-recognized degree may lead to legal complications, as students may have grounds to sue the government for misinformation and the time and money invested in pursuing an invalid degree.

If a student holds a work permit, they have the flexibility to pursue any degree. The Statement of Purpose (SOP) plays a crucial role in the application process for non-immigrant visas. In this document, the student needs to articulate the educational purpose convincingly. When applying for a non-immigrant visa, it is essential to persuade the immigration officer about the course's relevance to the student's career future plans, and how it represents a sound investment in terms of time and money. The student must assure the visa officer that the acquired degree will contribute to their growth and that they intend to return to their home country post-education. Validity of the degree is a critical factor in building this persuasive case. Our guidance to students is aimed at ensuring they make informed choices, avoid wasting time and money, and maintain realistic expectations throughout the application process.

Studying International Medicine Abroad

India faces a substantial demand for doctors, estimated at approximately 500,000, while the country can produce a maximum of 50,000 to 80,000 doctors annually. The visible difference in setting up medical colleges compared to engineering colleges amplifies the scarcity of medical seats. With approximately 20 lakh students attempting the UG NEET (National Eligibility cum Entrance Test) for undergraduate medical courses, only a maximum of 100,000 students can secure admission. This leaves a vast majority, around 19 lakh aspirants, seeking alternative options or leading them to explore opportunities in medical institutes outside India.

Countries such as Russia, Ukraine, Georgia, the Philippines, Kyrgyzstan, Kazakhstan, and Uzbekistan offer bachelor's degrees in medicine at a relatively lower cost. However, these degrees don't automatically grant registration to practice as a doctor in those countries as well as in India. To validate their certificates in India, students must undergo the FMG (Foreign Medical Graduate) Examination. Starting from 2028, this examination will be known as NEXT (National Exit Test). Following successful completion of this test, students are required to undergo a one-year internship before being allowed to practice medicine in India.

However, the success rate in this context is below 20%, primarily attributed to the quality of education or students struggling to achieve success in the FMG (Foreign Medical Graduate) examination. When students with a 50% score pursue medicine, it has the potential to impact the overall quality. These medical colleges often have lenient admission criteria, lack essential infrastructural and clinical facilities, and offer a curriculum with a much lower fee structure compared to Indian standards. The shortage of qualified lecturers further compounds the challenges. The result is a frustrating situation for students who, after investing 6-7 years of time and money, find themselves unable to clear the FMG exam.

Therefore, my advice is for students considering medicine in another country to thoroughly assess whether they will be eligible to practice in that specific country. Unfortunately, many parents overlook this crucial aspect due to the ease of admission, lower criteria, and reduced fees, ultimately leading to widespread frustration among students.

Undergraduate Medical Education Abroad

In recent years, there has been a noticeable increase in the number of students opting to pursue undergraduate medical degrees abroad. The allure of lower tuition fees often attracts both parents and students to explore foreign medical schools. However, it is essential to underscore that prioritizing the quality of education should be paramount when embarking on a career as noble as medicine.

The decision to pursue medical education abroad is frequently driven by the limited availability of seats in domestic medical colleges. For example, in India alone, approximately 2,000,000 students take the UG NEET exam annually, while medical colleges can only accommodate 5% of them. This means that 95%

of aspiring students are unable to secure admissions despite the pressing need for doctors in a densely populated country.

Moreover, even among the 5% who secure seats in Indian medical colleges, around 50% are compelled to pay exorbitant fees for admission to private medical institutions. This high cost poses a significant barrier for many middle-class families seeking to support their children's aspirations of becoming doctors.

Studying Post Graduation in Medicine

Attaining post-graduate medical education from prestigious institutions overseas is a common ambition among numerous medical students today. For those unable to secure specialization admission in their home countries, pursuing advanced studies in nations like the USA and UK presents an attractive option. Despite having earned their bachelor's degree in medicine, these students face specific eligibility requirements when aiming to pursue their master's degree abroad.

In nations such as the United States, achieving success in the USMLE (United States Medical Licensing Examination) is compulsory, whereas in the UK, candidates are required to pass the PLAB (Professional and Linguistic Assessments Board) exam, also known as MLA (Medical Licensing Assessment). These standardized assessments, aimed at evaluating candidates' medical knowledge and skills, typically need to be completed post-MBBS in India or after the third year of an undergraduate degree. It's important to highlight that examination centers are located in various countries, including India, facilitating accessibility for students undertaking these evaluations.

Nevertheless, passing these exams represents just one phase in the process of pursuing a master's degree (residency) abroad. In addition to the exams, candidates must acquire local clinical experience and procure endorsements from medical experts in the respective countries to secure a residency position. Moreover, advanced-level exams like USMLE Step 3 and PLAB 2 are exclusively available within their respective countries, necessitating aspirants to explore temporary immigration and visa options to undertake these exams or participate in clinical training.

Certainly, this process poses challenges, demands extensive time and effort, and incurs substantial expenses. Aspirants must invest significant resources in preparing for and successfully passing these exams. Nevertheless, it's crucial to recognize that upon completion, physicians in these countries enjoy lucrative salaries and abundant opportunities for career advancement and professional growth.

Embarking on post-graduate medical studies abroad represents a challenging yet fulfilling journey. The dedication, perseverance, and financial commitment required to fulfill the rigorous criteria are directed towards enjoying the rewards of a thriving medical career in these nations.

When contemplating a medical school abroad, it is crucial for both students and parents to evaluate specific criteria, including:

1. Is the medical school listed in the world directory of medical schools?

2. Does the medical school have a hospital for clinical practice?

3. What is the success rate of the medical school? How many students successfully obtain a license to practice medicine?

4. Does the country provide a medical license to practice medicine for graduates?

5. Does the medical school offer specialized studies, such as postgraduate courses in medicine or surgery for international students?

6. Are there examinations that students must pass to practice medicine in both their home country and the host country?

7. What is the success rate of these exams for graduates of the specific medical school?

8. What is the medium of instruction, and what is the local language in that country?

Countries like the USA, UK, Australia, and New Zealand maintain stringent standards of medical education. However, admission to undergraduate medicine programs in these countries often requires certain criteria and exams. While the educational quality is commendable, the cost for foreign students can be prohibitive, posing challenges for middle-class families.

As a result, students and families may consider countries such as Russia, Ukraine, Kazakhstan, Kyrgyzstan, China, and Georgia, which offer medical education at a significantly lower cost. Nevertheless, adherence to the aforementioned criteria is crucial, as these countries may not consistently provide the same level of education and clinical exposure as higher-cost countries.

It's worth noting that there is an affordable pathway for students aspiring to practice medicine in the United States through Caribbean medical schools and universities. These institutions offer quality education alongside clinical practice opportunities in the USA. However, the cost for this pathway is higher than that of lower-budget countries mentioned earlier, yet it remains notably lower than direct admission to medical schools in the USA.

In conclusion, it is advisable for parents and students to carefully evaluate all eight parameters before selecting medical schools abroad to pursue an undergraduate degree in medicine. This meticulous approach ensures that the quality of education aligns with the noble profession of medicine and the future aspirations of the students.

PROCESS OF APPLICATION

Profile Assessment

A prevalent trend among students pursuing higher education abroad is an undue emphasis on the ranking of universities, often at the expense of adequately evaluating their own academic profile. Each institution has specific admission criteria, typically considering factors such as GPA, statement of purpose (SOP), language proficiency, and standardized test scores, educational gap, backlogs for candidate selection.

However, many students apply indiscriminately to numerous universities, numbering anywhere from 20 to 50, only to find themselves consistently overlooked for admission. This pattern frequently results in disillusionment, with individuals concluding erroneously that they are inherently unsuitable for enrollment anywhere.

Contrary to such perceptions, the pivotal aspect lies in meticulously assessing one's own academic credentials and aligning them with the admission prerequisites of target universities. Thus, a comprehensive profile evaluation becomes imperative for aspirants seeking to pursue higher education overseas.

Entry Requirement, Acceptance Rate, Consulting, & Selecting Universities

Students should evaluate their academic grades, records, and language proficiency to ascertain their suitability for higher education abroad. Consulting an educational advisor and candidly discussing both their requirements and limitations is highly recommended. Concealing limitations can hinder accurate diagnosis and subsequent guidance.

Profile assessment is the cornerstone of this process, and it is best conducted by individuals with extensive experience in evaluating students against the acceptance criteria of various universities. Relying solely on guidance from alumni or current students may not provide comprehensive insights, as they may lack the breadth of experience necessary to understand diverse student profiles and university criteria. Therefore, students are advised to seek guidance from experienced professionals who can provide tailored solutions based on accurate information. Concealing facts may lead to inappropriate solutions, underscoring the importance of transparency in providing accurate guidance to students.

Transparency with the consultant or counselor is essential. Instead of applying to a multitude of universities, focusing on 2-5 carefully selected options recommended by the consultant or counselor can streamline the admission process, saving time, money, and frustration. This way would certainly lead to positive outcomes.

Application Deadline

The majority of universities operate on two main intake periods:

- The Fall intake - Occurring in September and October.

- The Spring intake - Spanning from January to March.

- The Summer intake - Spanning from May to July, although this is not universally available.

Each intake is associated with specific application deadlines. Applying early may yield benefits such as early bird scholarships and greater ease in securing admission and university accommodation. Conversely, last-minute applications can result in costly accommodation arrangements.

To avoid such challenges, students should initiate the application process well in advance. Delays in visa processing can lead to missed intakes, potentially resulting in a year-long setback. Additionally, last-minute visa approvals may incur substantial expenses, including inflated flight fares, transportation costs to the institute, and temporary accommodation expenses until permanent arrangements are made.

Completing all prerequisites early, including language proficiency tests, academic transcripts, and letters of recommendation, is crucial to avoid delays in the application process. Professors are encouraged to provide letters of recommendation promptly to expedite the application timeline.

Early preparation and timely submission of all required documents are vital to mitigate potential setbacks and ensure a smooth transition into university life.

Language Proficiency/Entrance Exams

Language proficiency is a crucial factor for students planning to pursue higher education abroad, particularly when the medium of instruction differs from their native language. English-speaking countries like the US, UK, Australia, New Zealand, and Canada typically require proficiency tests such as TOEFL, IELTS, Duolingo, or PTE, depending on the specific course and degree level.

Conversely, European countries may have courses taught in English, but local languages are prevalent, leading to potential language barriers. While professors often provide translations, students may struggle to fully comprehend lectures delivered in their native language. Countries such as Germany, France, Denmark, Finland, Italy, Spain, Sweden, Poland, Lithuania, Latvia, Kyrgyzstan, and Russia primarily use their local languages for the courses. To effectively communicate with faculty and enhance internship and job prospects, proficiency in the local language is essential for students intending to study in these countries.

Gre Exams

In the United States and Canada, GRE scores are typically required for admission to STEM graduate programs. However, some universities in these countries may offer admission without GRE scores. Conversely, countries such as Australia, the UK, Ireland, and New Zealand do not require GRE exams for admission.

For undergraduate courses in the US and Canada, SAT scores are commonly required. In contrast, universities in the UK, New Zealand, Ireland, and Australia typically assess applicants based on their GPA rather than SAT scores.

Documents Sop, Letter of Recommendation, and Other Documentation

If you meet the GPA criteria, the admissions committee will review your Statement of Purpose (SOP). They will assess why you have chosen their university, why the selected course aligns with your goals, why studying in that specific country is advantageous, and how the course will benefit you. If you satisfy these requirements, admission is achievable.

- **Letter of Recommendation**

The quality of the letter of recommendation is a crucial factor. These recommendations should be given by your teachers, lecturers, professors, or your employer/manager in case you are working. But at least one academic recommendation is mandatory in most of the education institutions.

– Any gaps or drops in the student's academic record must be justified with a written affidavit submitted to the university.

– All documents must adhere to the university's specific requirements. While some institutions may prefer physical documents, others may opt for online submission, particularly in light of the COVID-19 pandemic. Additionally, certain countries, including some Caribbean nations and European countries, may require documents to be apostilled by the external affairs ministry.

– Students should carefully consider these requirements and ensure that all necessary documents are collected at least six to nine months prior to the start of the course, depending on the destination country of higher education.

– Admission can be pursued even without final results, with the student receiving a conditional admission letter from the university. In the case of undergrad admissions, a predicted scorecard plays an important role in countries like the UK and USA.

Credentials

Various countries utilize distinct grading systems, necessitating applicants to adhere to the grading requirements specific to each country and institute. To facilitate this process, designated agencies such as WES (World Education Services) or NARIC have been appointed. Students are required to submit their transcripts, which include statements of marks and the number of hours devoted to studying each subject, to these agencies for evaluation. Subsequently, the agencies provide a detailed assessment report indicating the suitability of the applicant's profile for their desired course, university, or country of application.

- **Funding Resources**

Regarding funding, when applying for visas or university admission, institutions typically require proof of funds for tuition and accommodation. These funds must be maintained in accounts belonging to the student or their parents; accounts held by distant relatives are not accepted in most countries. Students must be prepared to provide documentation demonstrating the source of their funds.

- **Visa/Mock Interview**

Obtaining a visa after securing admission to a university is a critical step, as it determines whether the student can commence or complete their course physically. It's imperative to meticulously prepare all necessary documents for the visa application, seeking professional assistance from education consultants. Reliance solely on information from friends or alumni is discouraged, as visa regulations are subject to frequent changes.

In some countries, visa interviews are conducted, and the outcome depends on the applicant's performance. To familiarize themselves with the interview process, students should undergo 5-6 mock interviews to anticipate potential questions and learn how to respond effectively. Education consultants play a crucial role in guiding and preparing students for these visa interviews.

Agreement Between Students and University

When students pursue education abroad, they typically agree to a specific fee structure outlined by international universities. This agreement is governed by the Student Protection Law, which ensures that students are entitled to a refund of fees if they encounter dissatisfaction with the institution or encounter visa issues.

Within this agreement, attendance is often a stipulated requirement. Failure to meet attendance requirements may result in the termination of a student's admission, revocation of their visa, and in some cases, the non-refund of fees. It is crucial for students to thoroughly review and adhere to the details outlined in this agreement/refund policy, particularly regarding fees, attendance, discipline, and potential disciplinary actions.

Payment to University and Third Parties

When paying university fees, it's advisable to do so from a native account, whether it belongs to the student or their parents. Using a relative's account in the destination country could potentially lead to visa complications, as it might suggest intentions of immigration. Furthermore, in the event of a refund requirement in the future, the funds would typically be disbursed to the same native account. Involving a third party could introduce unnecessary complications.

Pick Up and Drop Arrangements

Many universities offer pickup and drop services, which may be complimentary or subject to a fee, depending on the university's policy. Students should inform the university at least 48 hours in advance if they wish to avail themselves of this service, providing their flight details. Alternatively, students can opt out of this service by notifying the university accordingly.

SIM Card

It is essential for students to obtain a SIM card upon arrival in the destination country to facilitate communication with their families back home. Nowadays, it is also possible to carry a SIM card from their home country for the destination country. While internet facilities are available at airports, compatibility issues may arise with international phones. Having a local SIM card ensures seamless communication. It is advisable to have your resume readily available with contact details upon arrival so that you can begin job applications immediately and provide your local contact number. Before purchasing a SIM card, students should carefully review available plans to select one that best suits their usage needs.

Opening a Bank Account

It is essential to have a bank account to receive payments from your part-time job employer. In some countries, you may have the option to open a bank account in your home country, which can be convenient. If this option is not available, you can obtain a letter from your educational institution and open a bank account in the destination country within a week. A bank account also serves as proof of address. When selecting a bank, consider various offers such as credit card offers and cash-back deals. Opt for a free account over a chargeable one, as some banks may impose fees for account opening and maintenance.

INSURANCE

Medical Insurance

It is essential to have both medical and wealth insurance when traveling to foreign countries. Medical insurance is particularly crucial as healthcare costs abroad can be exorbitant, with a single visit to a general practitioner potentially costing hundreds of dollars. Therefore, it is imperative to obtain medical insurance before embarking on your journey. Some institutions have preferred insurance partners, and they may require you to contact these companies for coverage. Medical insurance can provide coverage for various health issues throughout the year, offering peace of mind for international students. Additionally, some countries may require payment of a health surcharge during the visa application process, ensuring coverage for any health-related issues through their designated agency.

Wealth Insurance

When considering private or shared accommodation options, it is advisable to inquire whether the landlord has wealth insurance. This insurance should cover the tenants' belongings in case of theft or fire, providing necessary protection for personal assets. In many cases, wealth insurance is mandatory for tenants, ensuring financial security in unforeseen circumstances.

Connecting with Senior Students

Building connections with senior students who are studying in the same area and university is highly recommended. Their insights and guidance can be invaluable, and they may even assist you in finding part-time job and internship opportunities. Senior students can offer valuable advice on various aspects such as local offers, opportunities, safety, and transportation options. Consult multiple senior students to gather diverse perspectives and make informed decisions. Additionally, seek assistance from counselors or academic advisors at the university if you have any questions or concerns.

Taking Part-Time Jobs

Many countries permit students to work part-time while pursuing their studies, with varying criteria depending on the country. However, it is advisable not to rush into taking up employment immediately upon arrival. Beginning work within the first week may hinder your ability to explore the city, interact with locals and fellow students, familiarize yourself with the university, and becoming used to with new system.

We recommend allocating at least a month to acclimate yourself to the local area, engage with peers, and discover nearby places of interest. This initial period is crucial for gaining knowledge and making informed decisions after seeking advice. Subsequently, you can comfortably balance work and study commitments, becoming more deeply involved in both aspects of student life.

Engaging in part-time employment offers invaluable exposure and financial independence. It allows you to learn the importance of financial management while also expanding your professional network beyond the confines of your educational institution. Professionals you meet during part-time work may provide references for future full-time job opportunities, proving to be immensely beneficial for international students.

Work Culture

The work culture in foreign countries often diverges from that of many Asian nations.

Firstly, once working hours conclude, individuals typically aren't answerable to any superior. However, punctuality remains paramount in these settings.

Payment structures commonly involve weekly or bi-weekly disbursements, especially in larger corporations. Employers bear the responsibility of deducting taxes before transferring wages to employees, necessitating possession of a tax number (For Example -SSN in USA & NI in UK) for seamless payment processing.

Regarding professional conduct, scheduling appointments with relevant parties or clients well in advance is customary. Additionally, it's advisable to ensure preparedness and completion of necessary tasks at least 15-20 minutes before the scheduled appointment time.

Finding Accommodation

International students have various options for accommodation, but caution is advised when using online portals as some may be unreliable.

University Accommodation

University accommodation is often the best choice, with dormitories offering affordable and convenient living arrangements. Dormitories foster a sense of community among students and provide essential amenities in a safe environment.

Alternatively, students may opt for halls, which offer single-bedded accommodations with private bathrooms and kitchen facilities. However, these tend to be more expensive.

Homestays

Homestay arrangements allow students to live with local families, providing an immersive cultural and linguistic experience. Universities and immigration authorities typically establish criteria for homestay arrangements, ensuring the safety and well-being of students.

Private Accommodations

Private accommodation, recommended by educational institutions, works on monthly rent payments without meal options. Students are responsible for cooking, cleaning, and managing their living space.

Shared accommodations

Shared accommodations involve multiple students renting a house together and sharing expenses. While this option may be suitable for mature students, hostels or homestays are recommended for those in their early years of study.

AVAILABILITY OF FINANCIAL AID, SCHOLARSHIP, BURSARY, EDUCATIONAL LOANS AVAILABLE

Scholarships

Many scholarships are available, but the deadline is before the deadline of the course application. Students have to keep in mind and apply for scholarships sooner because until they get an admission letter, their scholarships cannot be processed.

While navigating through these challenges can be daunting, it is entirely manageable with initiative-taking planning.

Financial support for international students typically comes in two forms: scholarships and assistantships. It comes from foreign governments, organizations, individual courses, or Commonwealth Scholarship.

Numerous scholarships are accessible, yet they often have deadlines preceding the application deadlines for courses. Therefore, students must be mindful of this and apply for scholarships well in advance. It's crucial to note that scholarship applications cannot be processed until students receive their admission letters.

Bursary

Students who demonstrate academic excellence, sincerity, and a genuine interest in a specific course may have the opportunity to receive bursaries if they successfully convince the admission committee of their merits. However, it's important to note that individuals with backlogs or lower grades shouldn't be discouraged from pursuing studies abroad. In such cases, applying for education loans is a viable option.

Fortunately, many banks now offer education loans to support students in financing their studies abroad. These loans can amount to as much as one crore rupees. By consulting with educational advisors during the loan application process, students can receive guidance on which banks provide loans based on their academic scores, preferred university, and course of study. This approach helps streamline the process and minimize potential complications.

Education Loan and Recommendations

Many students and parents are considering education loans as part of their financial strategy for studying abroad.

Certain Indian banks provide education loans without requiring collateral up to a certain limit, but collateral becomes mandatory for amounts exceeding this threshold. Government banks typically offer lower interest rates compared to commercial and private banks. Banks assess the earning capacity of the family, excluding the student. It's important to note that if the student is currently employed, their salary might not be accessible once their course begins.

Before applying for an education loan, it's advisable to consult with an education consultant or financial institution to assess your eligibility. Additionally, exploring more flexible financial institutions where your profile aligns well can expedite the approval process with minimal delays.

Assistantship

Additionally, students can apply for assistantships while studying. These programs allow students to work in areas such as the college library, cultural committees, or group study sessions, and receive payment that may offset tuition fees. To qualify for assistantships, students need an excellent GPA and the physical capability to balance work responsibilities with their studies.

Free Education in International Institutions

Numerous advertisements on social media tout "FREE EDUCATION" at institutes abroad, may entice students. However, it's essential to understand that free education in these countries typically comes with specific criteria, notably instruction in the local language rather than English.

Many European institutes offer such programs, but they often have stringent entry requirements, and courses are taught in the local language. Therefore, proficiency in the local language is necessary before applying. Pathways are available to facilitate admission for students interested in these programs. These pathways involve completing a paid program that prepares students up to the B-level of the local language, enabling them to transition to the principal program, which is entirely tuition-free. Although students must invest an additional year and pay fees for the preparatory education, the bachelor's or master's degree program is completely free.

Rules and Regulations

Pre-Departure Briefing and Awareness

Here's a quick overview of the further procedures:

1. Flight Ticket and Accommodation Booking:

– Secure your flight ticket and accommodation as soon as possible.

2. Airport Pickup Assistance:

– If you require assistance with airport pickup, please send your flight ticket at least 72 hours in advance.

3. Assistance Services:

– Reach out in advance if you need assistance with obtaining an international mobile SIM, foreign exchange, or a Forex card.

4. International Student Card:

– Book your international student card promptly to benefit from various discounts abroad.

5. University/College Documents:

– Collect necessary documents from your university or college.

6. Packing Essentials:

– Review the list of items to carry abroad and select according to your needs.

These steps will help streamline your transition and ensure a smooth start to your international student experience.

Things to Check Before Leaving for the Destination Country

Upon arrival in a new country, it's important to familiarize yourself with certain things. I recommend allowing at least a month to adjust to the new system and environment.

1. Currency Card and Local Currency:

– Collect your international currency card/open a bank account in the destination country and carry a debit card with exchanged currency for the destination country.

2. Pick-up and Drop Arrangements:

– Confirm pick-up and drop-off arrangements with your institute at least 72 hours before your flight.

3. Arrival Time at Airport:

– Arrive at the airport at least three hours before your flight departure.

– Check for transit visa requirements for layovers.

4. Documentation:

– Carry original academic and financial documents, passport, admission letter (I20/CEO/CAS), and visa.

– Keep documents accessible and cooperate with Immigration officials.

5. Communication and Connectivity:

– Bring your resume and ensure you have a mobile SIM card.

– If international roaming is unavailable, purchase a local SIM upon arrival.

– Utilize airport internet facilities for WhatsApp communication with family.

6. University International Office:

– Report to the university's international office promptly upon arrival.

7. Academic Documents and Student ID:

– Collect all required documents, including your student ID, as per the provided list.

8. Accommodation Confirmation:

– Confirm accommodation booking and ensure a tenancy agreement with the landlord.

9. Work Regulations:

– Adhere to the 20-hour per week work limit.

– Monitor work hours to avoid exceeding the limit.

Adhering to these instructions will facilitate a smooth transition for your study abroad journey.

Code of Conduct

Before embarking on a journey abroad for higher education, it's paramount to acquaint oneself with the rules and regulations that govern various aspects of student life. Comprehending and adhering to these regulations is not only necessary for compliance but also for facilitating a seamless and enjoyable academic endeavor. Here are key considerations to bear in mind before pursuing further studies overseas:

1. Insurance Regulations:

International students must pay close attention to the insurance requirements stipulated by their host country. Many nations mandate health insurance coverage for students, necessitating a thorough understanding of the specified criteria. Familiarizing oneself with the intricacies of the healthcare system and insurance provisions in the host country can aid in navigating potential medical issues smoothly.

2. Discount Student Card Regulations:

Numerous countries offer discount cards for students, entitling them to various benefits such as reduced fares on public transportation and discounted entry to cultural sites. It's essential for students to acquaint themselves with the eligibility criteria and application process for obtaining these cards, as they can significantly alleviate living expenses.

3. Work Regulations During Studies:

While pursuing studies abroad, many international students seek part-time employment to support their living costs. However, understanding the regulations governing work permits, permissible work hours, and employment restrictions is imperative. Adhering to these regulations is crucial to avoid legal repercussions that could jeopardize one's residency in the host country.

4. Privacy Policy Regulations:

Familiarizing oneself with the privacy and data protection laws of the host country is indispensable, particularly concerning financial transactions, housing arrangements, and academic records. Awareness of these regulations empowers students to safeguard their personal information and ensure compliance with local legislation.

5. Awareness About Other Regulations:

In addition to the aforementioned aspects, it's essential for international students to be cognizant of various other regulations, encompassing visa requirements, housing regulations, academic integrity policies, and emergency procedures. Staying informed about these regulations facilitates students' adaptation to their new environment and mitigates the risk of unintentional breaches.

Prior to commencing their international educational journey, students are advised to conduct comprehensive research and familiarize themselves with the rules and regulations pertinent to their specific circumstances. Seeking guidance from the educational institution, relevant government agencies, or seasoned professionals such as education counselors and consultants can provide invaluable insights and ensure a rewarding and successful academic experience abroad.

Country Regulations

When students venture abroad, it's imperative to adhere meticulously to the distinct rules and regulations of each country, particularly as an international student holding a non-immigrant visa.

- This includes strict compliance with attendance policies set forth by the university. Failure to meet these attendance requirements may prompt the university to notify the immigration office, which retains the authority to revoke your study visa. It's crucial to exercise caution and diligently follow the instructions provided during your orientation session and outlined on the institute's official website.

- Timely payment of fees is essential. Failure to meet financial clearance requirements may result in the university terminating your admission, subsequently invalidating your visa. In such a scenario, you would be required to leave the country, as non-compliance could lead to deportation.

Respect for local customs and regulations is paramount. Informing neighbors prior to hosting parties with loud music is necessary to avoid potential police intervention. *Once while visiting the United Kingdom, I encountered a remarkable family in the local neighborhood. The woman, who was separated, resided with her boyfriend and her daughter from her previous marriage. On a particular day when her daughter fell ill, her ex-husband came to stay over to care for the child. It struck me as extraordinary that both her ex-husband and current boyfriend lived harmoniously under the same roof. Coming from the traditional Indian family structure, this arrangement seemed quite unconventional to me. It made me reflect on the importance of prioritizing humanity over societal norms and fostering healthy relationships. This incident highlights the diverse cultural experiences that students may encounter when studying abroad. Embracing and respecting the customs of the host country can facilitate quicker integration and adjustment.*

- Additionally, littering and spitting on roads are strictly prohibited, as surveillance cameras may capture such actions, leading to repercussions.

Case of Urinating on the Sidewalk

A student studying overseas was fined $100 for urinating on the sidewalk. While it might be a casual thing to do in India, his impatience attracted a heavy fine.

Students need to be mindful of the country they are going to and the local regulations. When you are going as a student, you are representing your country and your country's image. Getting indulged in such infamy can create a wrong impression not only for the student but also for his home country.

- Engaging in activities that trouble local minors under 18, or violating laws concerning their well-being can land international students in legal trouble. It's imperative to recognize that minors are under governmental protection, and any disregard for their safety or welfare is not tolerated.

- Before traveling to the United States of America, it's crucial to ensure compliance with fee payment regulations. At the immigration desk, officers may inquire about your admission fee payment and financial status and request relevant documentation. Failure to demonstrate payment of university fees could result in admission cancellation, visa revocation, and potential deportation.

- Regarding healthcare, access to the medical system is contingent upon registration with a local general practitioner, regardless of possessing medical insurance. Upon arrival in the destination country, promptly registering with a general practitioner in your residing area is advisable to facilitate medical care. Similarly, accessing medical treatment in a foreign country typically requires an appointment, even in emergency situations. However, if faced with an urgent medical need, expressing the urgency of the situation may facilitate obtaining the earliest available appointment for emergency treatment.

- The student visa typically permits part-time work, often restricted to 20 hours per week. However, some students may encounter employers offering opportunities exceeding these limitations, sometimes paying in cash. Engaging in such arrangements poses significant risks, as discovery by immigration authorities could result in immediate deportation.

- Furthermore, exceeding the permissible work hours stipulated by the visa conditions may jeopardize future visa extensions or transitions, such as switching from a study visa to a work permit. This could impede eligibility for post-study work visas, even upon successful course completion. Students must exercise caution and refrain from accepting work offers exceeding their visa restrictions.

- Additionally, it's essential for students to proactively manage visa-related matters, such as applying for extensions or visa transitions, well in advance, ideally at least a month before the current visa's expiration.

- Moreover, students should adopt a cautious approach when interacting with strangers, refraining from accepting offers of transportation or drinks to ensure their safety and well-being.

Work Culture

The work culture in foreign countries often diverges from that of many Asian nations.

Firstly, once working hours conclude, individuals typically aren't answerable to any superior. However, punctuality remains paramount in these settings.

Payment structures commonly involve weekly or bi-weekly disbursements, especially in larger corporations. Employers bear the responsibility of deducting taxes before transferring wages to employees, necessitating possession of a tax number for seamless payment processing.

Regarding professional conduct, scheduling appointments with relevant parties or clients well in advance is customary. Additionally, it's advisable to ensure preparedness and completion of necessary tasks at least 15-20 minutes before the scheduled appointment time.

VISA

Immigration Rules

When students venture abroad, it's imperative to adhere meticulously to the distinct rules and regulations of each country, particularly as an international student holding a non-immigrant visa.

This includes strict compliance with attendance policies set forth by the university. Failure to meet these attendance requirements may prompt the university to notify the immigration office, which retains the authority to revoke your study visa. It's crucial to exercise caution and diligently follow the instructions provided during your orientation session, which are outlined on the institute's official website.

Timely payment of fees is essential. Failure to meet financial clearance requirements may result in the university terminating your admission, subsequently invalidating your visa. In such a scenario, you would be required to leave the country, as non-compliance could lead to deportation.

Respect for local customs and regulations is paramount. Informing neighbors prior to hosting parties with loud music is necessary to avoid potential police intervention.

- Additionally, littering and spitting on roads are strictly prohibited, as surveillance cameras may capture such actions, leading to repercussions.

- Engaging in activities that trouble local minors under 18, or violating laws concerning their well-being, can land international students in legal trouble. It's imperative to recognize that minors are under governmental protection, and any disregard for their safety or welfare is not tolerated.

- Before traveling to the United States of America, it's crucial to ensure compliance with fee payment regulations. At the immigration desk, officers may inquire about your admission fee payment, financial status, and request relevant documentation. Failure to demonstrate payment of university fees could result in admission cancellation, visa revocation, and potential deportation.

- Regarding healthcare, access to the medical system is contingent upon registration with a local general practitioner, regardless of possessing medical insurance. Upon arrival in the destination country, promptly registering with a general practitioner in your residing area is advisable to facilitate medical care. Similarly, accessing medical treatment in a foreign country typically requires an appointment, even in emergency situations. However, if faced with an urgent medical need, expressing the urgency of the situation may facilitate obtaining the earliest available appointment for emergency treatment.

- The student visa typically permits part-time work, often restricted to 20 hours per week. However, some students may encounter employers offering opportunities exceeding these limitations, sometimes paying in cash. Engaging in such arrangements poses significant risks, as discovery by immigration authorities could result in immediate deportation. Furthermore, exceeding the permissible work hours stipulated by the visa conditions may jeopardize future visa extensions or transitions, such as switching from a study visa to a work permit. This could impede eligibility for post-study work visas, even upon successful course completion. Students must exercise caution and refrain from accepting work offers exceeding their visa restrictions.

- Additionally, it's essential for students to proactively manage visa-related matters, such as applying for extensions or visa transitions well in advance, ideally at least a month before the current visa's expiration.

- Moreover, students should adopt a cautious approach when interacting with strangers, refraining from accepting offers of transportation or drinks, to ensure their safety and well-being.

WHY IMMIGRATON CAN DENY YOUR VISA?

When it comes to studying abroad, students must be aware of the immigration rules. Most students and parents are not aware of the policies regarding studying abroad. A student should keep in mind that there are two important aspects to studying abroad:

1. Getting admission to the desired program

2. Admission to the country

Most countries like the UK, the US, Australia, and New Zealand set rules for Asian students. When they receive applications from Asian students, the first thing they consider is whether the person is a potential immigrant and what their long-term plans are for staying in the country. After the completion of the post-study visa, when a student applies for a post-study visa, it's a non-immigrant visa, and their purpose is solely to study there. However, most students are not aware of this. Students should not depend on working and making money; they need to focus on their studies.

Eligibility for a Course

Consider a student who has completed a higher degree—masters and is applying for a diploma. There are several questions about why the student is opting for lower-level education in the same subject. So, it's considered that the major intention is not to study but to pay a small fee and settle in the country.

One lady came and told me, "I am a doctor and have completed my degree in India. Now, I do not want to pursue higher education in medicine; I want to opt for a course in fashion design abroad." It is not very easy to get admission to creative art courses. You need to show that you have done that kind of work before, and your portfolio is required. This applies to all creative art subjects. So, this transition is difficult. We advise them to think about how easy/difficult a subject could be. It is also difficult to convince the university. Sometimes, the university might give admission, but it's difficult to get a visa in such circumstances. And unless the visa is received, the student cannot go to the country and pursue the course.

While opting for a course, a student should consider that if they are a diploma holder, they can opt for an advanced diploma. If they are a graduate, they can opt for masters, and if they are masters, they can opt for a PhD or an MBA.

Again, the immigration might ask you why you are not taking this course in your country. What is the difference between pursuing the course in India and the US?

Many students say the course content is different and more practical. In fact, students can say if they complete this course in India, they will be in the same environment which they have already experienced. However, if they study in the US, the teaching/learning style will be different. Again, there will be students from different countries, and they can exchange their thoughts with them. And in a true manner, they will get international exposure if they complete it from a foreign country. If you fail to answer this properly, there is a chance your visa will be denied.

Managing Funding

Students and parents need to show the bank balance that would suffice their tuition fee and stay while in the destination country.

Recently, 6-7 students were deported from the US. They got a US visa and went to the US where they were asked to show the receipt of their paid university fees. The students had not paid the fees, and they were asked what document they submitted for the visa. The immigration officer hen asked them to log in to their bank account and show if they had the requisite funds in their bank account, which is a mandatory criterion. The students did not have money in their accounts. The immigration officer told them to send an email to the university and withdraw their admission. As soon as the university withdrew their admission, the immigration revoked their visa, and the students were deported back to their native country the next day.

Remember, obtaining a visa will not guarantee your entry into the country. You need to have foolproof evidence of all intentions, formalities, and receipts before travelling abroad. Additionally, your bank should have the mandatory funds in your account. Different countries have different criteria. Some countries require maintaining funds in the bank for 6 months, while others have criteria of 3 months, 1 month, or 28 days. Few countries accept 100% education loans, but some accept no more than 50% to 60% education loans. Furthermore, some countries accept bank accounts of only parents, while others accept those of distant relatives (uncles or aunts). Therefore, it is advisable to check all requirements and recent changes before submitting your application.

Visa Rules

Students should be aware different countries have different immigration rules, and students should take precautions. Even the rules keep changing, and thus, it is important that students check the immigration rules on authentic sites or take guidance from an education consultant.

All these shortcomings might lead to loss of your intake. Again, your visa fee is not refundable even if your visa application is unsuccessful. There are certain immigration rules- If students go to the border and an immigration officer asks about their intention to work, and if the answer is "Yes," the student could land him/her in trouble. The immigration officer will consider your primary focus is not study, and you are a potential immigrant, and it might result in deportation.

To avoid all these hiccups, students need guidance and consultation. What answers will lead you inside a country and what answers will deny you a visa needs to be considered.

- Insurance is an important matter as far as studying abroad is concerned. There are certain countries where if you have a valid visa and insurance at the time of entry, and you are not renewing the insurance, then that is considered an illegal activity. When the person goes for a visa extension, this factor could surface, and the person will be termed illegal and overstayed if the student thinks who can see me working here? Who would know? There are many desi places where they can take employment, and these places are willing to pay in cash. The student might be excited they are getting paid well. But, if the immigration officer checks and the person is caught, they will directly take the person to the airport and deport them to their home country. So students should be aware of all this. People can misguide you. Your parents have worked hard to make your education possible, and having such experiences can not only mean a waste of all your efforts but also a slim possibility of you never entering the country again. Think long-term. If you wish to extend your stay in the country or apply for permanent residency, it is ideal to have a clean slate with no illegal records.

- Forged documents could ban you for 5-10 years from the country. Unless you prove the documents are authentic, the ban will continue.

- Once deported, the case is considered a forgery, and it can again bring a ban on your entry.

Remember, admission is pointless if the visa is denied. It's a critical aspect to consider.

Post-Study Visa

To be eligible for the government-provided post-study work permit, certain conditions must be met:

1. Successful completion of the enrolled program at the bachelor's, master's, or PhD level is required. Failure to attain the necessary credits, complete the dissertation, or achieve satisfactory grades in specific modules will result in receiving a diploma or postgraduate diploma instead of the desired degree, rendering one ineligible for the post-study work visa. Therefore, students aspiring to work in the destination country must ensure timely and successful completion of all modules and the dissertation with all course requirements. Only then can they avail themselves of the post-study work visa opportunity, allowing them to seek employment in the country where they completed their education.

2. During the course of study, institutes typically allow students to have not more than a specific number of resits or backlogs. If a student exceeds this threshold, the university may take strict measures, potentially resulting in termination of admission or the student receiving only a diploma or postgraduate diploma certification instead of a bachelor's or master's degree.

However, if a student encounters genuine issues, such as health problems, they are required to submit a medical certificate. This certificate may grant them a semester gap, allowing them to repeat the entire program with approval from the institute. Failing to provide relevant documentation to substantiate attendance or academic difficulties may lead to disciplinary action from the university. Once the institute takes action, it becomes challenging to persuade them otherwise. Hence, it is imperative to submit required documents promptly to avoid adverse consequences.

Visa Transfer

When considering visa transfer or transitioning from a study visa to a work visa, students must ensure they meet all necessary conditions before applying. Seeking guidance from consultants or immigration advisers at the educational institution is advisable. Once the application is submitted, there is limited assistance available if the outcome from immigration authorities is unfavorable.

Parent's Visiting Students

For parents intending to visit their children, obtaining a visit visa is essential. They must secure an invitation from their child and demonstrate sufficient funds for travel and accommodation in the destination country, as well as proof of income in their home country. Visit visa duration varies, ranging from 90 days to 10 years depending on the regulations of each country. One cannot stay in the destination country on a visit visa for more than 180 days.

Parents visiting foreign countries are strictly prohibited from working or earning money. Any attempt to do so could lead to repercussions from immigration authorities, potentially resulting in consequences for both the parents and their child.

Spouse/Child/Parent Dependent Visa

When traveling abroad, if you attend gatherings and are introduced to new acquaintances who offer you a ride home or ask for a lift, it's crucial to verify their immigration visa status in that country. If caught by the police while commuting with individuals staying illegally, you could face deportation alongside them, with a potential ban on re-entry to that country for up to 10 years.

Spouse, children, and parents above 65 years of age can be considered dependents of the primary applicant in certain countries. Some countries allow dependents to apply for visas and reside with the student, provided there are sufficient funds to support them. However, restrictions may apply, such as allowing dependents only for specific courses like research or postgraduate programs, but not bachelor's degrees. Visa requirements and regulations vary by country, and it's advisable to seek guidance from immigration or educational consultants before applying.

Certain countries mandate specific certifications for dependent visa applications. For instance, some European countries require language proficiency certificates before applying for a dependent visa.

In some foreign countries, dependents may have the option to work part-time, while others may not permit any form of employment. Seeking professional advice before submitting a dependent visa application is recommended for specific guidance on work eligibility and other requirements.

IN-HOUSE OPPORTUNITIES WITH INDUSTRY SPECIALISTS, EXPERTS

Collaboration between technical institutions, universities, and industry experts is prevalent. This close partnership facilitates internship opportunities for students during their studies, allowing them to gain valuable hands-on experience. These internships also often offer academic credits. Moreover, students can enhance their professional reputation and secure reference letters from industry professionals, significantly bolstering their chances of securing desirable employment opportunities within the same industry or elsewhere.

When industries encounter challenges with their products, they often reach out to relevant departments within universities for resolution. Professors in the respective fields collaborate with students to address these issues, providing them with valuable hands-on experience, potentially involving research projects. Additionally, students may receive compensation for their contributions.

Many countries provide post-study work visas, with durations varying based on the country and the course completed. These visas allow graduates to seek employment and gain work experience in the country where they completed their higher education.

TIME MANAGEMENT

Effective time management is essential for success in all aspects of life. It not only aids in achieving goals but also minimizes stress and enhances overall productivity. One simple yet powerful strategy for managing time is to categorize tasks into four components at the start of each day:

1. Urgent and Important

2. Urgent but Non-Important

3. Non-Urgent but Important

4. Non-Urgent and Non-Important

Urgent & Important	Non-Urgent but Important
Urgent but Non-Important	Non-Urgent & Non-Important

Prioritizing tasks that fall under the category of urgent and important is crucial, as these demand immediate attention. Addressing these tasks first allows for efficient time management and reduces the pressure of impending deadlines. Subsequently, tasks categorized as urgent but non-important can be addressed before moving on to non-urgent yet important tasks. Lastly, tasks classified as non-urgent and non-important should be tackled last.

This structured approach enables individuals to handle pressing matters when they are most alert and energized, leaving ample time later in the day to manage less time-sensitive tasks with a clearer mindset and reduced stress. Adopting this method can lead to a more enjoyable work experience and a healthier work-life balance.

It's important to remember that effective time management not only facilitates task completion but also contributes to a more balanced and fulfilling life.

OVERSEAS EDUCATION - GOING WITHOUT SUPPORT AND GUIDANCE

Embarking overseas education without proper support and guidance can indeed be a challenging and potentially risky endeavor. The process involves various stages, each with its own set of complexities.

1. Selecting the University:

– Without guidance, researching and selecting the right university can be overwhelming. Considerations should include the program of interest, faculty reputation, campus facilities, and location. Researching rankings, employability, internship opportunities, suitability as an individual, alumni reviews, and industry connections can help in making informed decisions.

2. Cost Involved:

– Understanding and estimating the total cost of education is crucial. This includes tuition fees, living expenses, insurance, and miscellaneous costs. Lack of guidance may lead to overlooking potential scholarships or financial aid options.

3. Student Visa Rules:

– Navigating the intricacies of student visa rules is essential. This involves understanding eligibility criteria, required documentation, and application processes. Failure to comply with visa regulations can lead to legal issues and jeopardize the entire education plan.

4. Admission Process:

– Applying to foreign universities involves detailed application processes, including academic transcripts, letters of recommendation, and a well-crafted personal statement. Lack of guidance may result in submitting incomplete or inaccurate applications, reducing the chances of acceptance.

5. Documents:

– Gathering and authenticating necessary documents is a time-consuming process. This includes academic certificates, test scores, and financial statements. Without guidance, students might overlook specific document requirements, leading to delays or rejections.

6. Interview Preparation:

– Some universities require interviews as part of the admission process. Lack of preparation can negatively impact the chances of acceptance. Therefore, understanding potential questions and practicing responses is essential.

7. Timelines:

– Meeting application deadlines   are critical. Lack of awareness or mismanagement may lead to missed opportunities or deferred admissions. Having a clear timeline for each stage of the process is crucial.

8. Admission and Post-Admission Acceptance:

– Securing admission is just the beginning. Without support, understanding acceptance procedures, including fee payment and accommodation booking, can be challenging. Adjusting to a new educational environment and culture can be overwhelming without proper guidance.

9. Post-Landing Guidance:

– Arriving in a new country without a support system can be isolating. Understanding local culture, setting up bank accounts, and finding accommodation can be daunting. Lack of guidance may result in difficulties adapting to the new environment.

Undertaking overseas education without a support system poses significant challenges. It's advisable for prospective students to seek guidance from educational consultants, alumni networks, or online resources to navigate the complexities of the process and ensure a smoother transition into international education. Online information may not be applicable for a few individuals and in certain circumstances.

Solutions

Navigating the complexities of overseas education can indeed be overwhelming, but there are solutions and strategies to make the process smoother for both parents and students. Here's an elaborate breakdown:

- **Trust the Experts:**

– Educational consultants specialize in guiding students through the entire process, from university selection to visa applications. Rely on professionals who have experience and knowledge in the field to provide accurate information and valuable insights. If you find something that is diverting your attention, you can discuss it with your counselor and reach a conclusion.

- **Seek Advice:**

– Connect with alumni who have already pursued overseas education. Their experiences can offer valuable advice on university choices, cultural adjustments, and more. Online forums, social media groups, and informational interviews can also provide diverse perspectives. Also, do not ignore variations in circumstances and rules at that time and the current situation.

- **Do Your Research:**

– Empower yourself with knowledge about the universities, programs, and countries of interest. Research factors like rankings, faculty, and campus life. Understanding the visa process, admission requirements and cultural nuances will help you make informed decisions. Consider all these factors before making any decision.

- **Encourage Adjustment and Adaptation:**

– Preparing mentally for a new environment is crucial. Encourage a positive mindset and openness to different cultures. Recognize that adaptation takes time, and providing emotional support during the initial adjustment period is essential.

- **Train Students to Take Responsibilities:**

– Overseas education involves managing various responsibilities. Teach students essential life skills such as budgeting, time management, and problem-solving. Independence and self-reliance will contribute to a smoother transition to living and studying abroad.

- **Prepare for Challenges:**

– Acknowledge that challenges may arise but view them as opportunities for growth. Problem-solving and resilience are valuable skills that come with overcoming obstacles. Have open and honest communication with your child about potential challenges and how to address them.

- **Cultural Sensitivity Training:**

– Familiarize students with the cultural norms and practices of the host country. This can reduce cultural shock and facilitate better integration. Understanding and respecting cultural differences contribute to a more enriching educational experience.

- **Encourage Networking:**

– Building a network in the new environment is crucial. Encourage participation in student organizations, networking events, and social activities. A supportive community can make the transition more comfortable and enhance the overall experience.

- **Stay Informed and Involved:**

– Parents must stay engaged in their child's educational journey. Regular communication, both about academic and personal aspects, can foster a sense of security and support. Be aware of the resources available, including support services provided by the university or local community.

By combining trust in experts, seeking advice, conducting thorough research, and fostering key skills in students, the journey toward overseas education becomes a more manageable and enriching experience. Encouraging adaptability and responsibility empowers students to thrive in a new educational and cultural environment.

PROS AND CONS OF STUDYING ABROAD

Although studying abroad might look like an exciting proposition, it could create setbacks for students on different fronts. It is therefore recommended to carefully consider the following aspects of studying abroad and foster a mindset that is prepared to address any situation that comes along.

Pros:

1. Cultural Immersion: Residing in a foreign country can facilitate valuable cultural immersion and language acquisition.

2. Academic Opportunities: Gain access to esteemed universities and specialized programs unavailable domestically.

3. Personal Development: Foster independence, adaptability, and problem-solving skills through navigating a novel environment.

4. Networking: Establish international connections and expand your professional network on a global scale.

5. Travel Experiences: Seize the opportunity to explore diverse countries and broaden your worldview.

Cons:

1. Financial Burden: Studying abroad often entails substantial expenses, encompassing tuition fees, living costs, and travel expenditures.

2. Homesickness: Coping with separation from family and friends can pose emotional challenges.

3. Language Barrier: Adjusting to a foreign language and overcoming communication barriers may prove challenging.

4. Adaptation Struggles: Assimilating into a new education system and cultural norms can induce stress.

5. Visa and Legal Complexities: Navigating intricate visa regulations and legal matters in a foreign jurisdiction can be daunting.

It is essential to carefully evaluate these factors before committing to studying abroad. Consulting with an education consultant can provide valuable guidance in making informed decisions tailored to individual circumstances.

THE ROLE OF COUNSELORS

Education counselors play a vital role in guiding students through their academic and career decisions, offering expertise and support to help them make informed choices about their future endeavors. To excel in this role, counselors must possess a diverse range of qualities and skills that enable them to provide valuable advice and assistance to students.

In today's rapidly changing educational landscape, it is essential for education counselors to stay informed about the latest trends and advancements in the field of education. They should have a comprehensive understanding of various academic pathways, emerging career prospects, and evolving job market demands. Keeping up-to-date with developments in the field ensures that counselors can offer relevant and accurate guidance to students.

Moreover, when recommending specific courses or educational paths, counselors should be able to justify their suggestions with logical reasoning and evidence. They need to possess in-depth knowledge of the strengths and weaknesses of different educational programs, enabling them to explain why a particular course of study is suitable for a student and why others may not be as appropriate. This requires a thorough understanding of the available educational options and their relevance to students' individual needs.

However, it is crucial for education counselors to remain impartial and avoid being influenced by affiliations with specific educational institutions. While some counselors may have associations with certain institutions, they should prioritize students' best interests above all else.

This ethical approach ensures that counselors provide unbiased guidance, considering students' unique profiles and career aspirations without favoring any particular institution.

Furthermore, conducting comprehensive profile assessments is a key aspect of the education counselor's role. By evaluating students' strengths, weaknesses, interests, and career goals, a counselor can offer tailored recommendations for suitable courses, educational institutions, and even opportunities for studying abroad. This personalized approach enhances students' satisfaction and success in their chosen educational paths.

In conclusion, the role of an education counselor is pivotal in shaping students' academic and professional futures. To fulfill this role effectively, counselors must possess up-to-date knowledge, impartiality, logical reasoning, and the ability to conduct individualized assessments. By embodying these qualities, education counselors can provide invaluable guidance and support to students as they navigate their educational and career journeys.

PROGRESS IN COMFORT ZONE VS NON-COMFORT ZONE

When individuals are preoccupied with existing friendships, they may inadvertently limit their inclination to explore new contacts for networking. This tendency can result in a relatively confined contact sphere, where interactions largely revolve around familiar faces and established relationships. While these existing friendships offer comfort and familiarity, they may also hinder opportunities for personal growth and development.

Conversely, not having an established circle of friends presents an opportunity for significant personal growth. In such circumstances, individuals are prompted to embrace the chance to make new connections and expand their social network. This openness to new friendships opens doors to a fresh network of individuals from diverse backgrounds, each bringing their own unique knowledge, experiences, and perspectives to the table.

The absence of pre-existing connections serves as a catalyst for expanding social circles, facilitating interactions with individuals who may have previously been outside of one's immediate social sphere. These new friendships offer opportunities for enriching encounters and meaningful exchanges, broadening one's horizons and exposing them to new ideas, cultures, and opportunities for personal and professional development.

By actively seeking out new connections and embracing the opportunity to expand their social network, individuals can cultivate a more diverse and dynamic social circle. This not only enhances their social experiences but also fosters personal growth and development through varied interactions and enriching encounters with a wider range of individuals.

THE HIDDEN COSTS OF STUDYING ABROAD

Studying abroad holds immense appeal for countless students, offering the chance to immerse oneself in a new culture, language, and academic environment. However, amidst the excitement of pursuing education overseas, there lurk hidden expenses that often catch students off guard.

Foremost among these hidden costs is the financial burden of living in a foreign land. While tuition fees may be transparent, the day-to-day expenses, including accommodation, meals, transportation, and miscellaneous costs, can vary drastically depending on the destination. Many students are taken aback by the steep cost of living in certain cities or regions, leading to unexpected financial strain during their time abroad.

Another often-overlooked expense is the impact of currency exchange rates. Fluctuations in currency values can significantly alter the cost of tuition, living essentials, and travel expenses, necessitating careful budgeting to avoid financial surprises.

Furthermore, students venturing abroad may encounter unforeseen fees associated with visas, insurance, and administrative formalities. Visa applications, health coverage, and residency permits often come with additional charges that students may not have accounted for initially.

It is imperative for students planning to study abroad to conduct thorough research and budget meticulously to accommodate these hidden costs. By considering all potential expenses upfront and planning ahead, students can better prepare for a successful and financially manageable experience abroad.

One effective strategy for mitigating costs is to capitalize on early enrollment discounts offered by universities. Many institutions extend discounts on tuition fees for students who apply and enroll ahead of schedule. Initiating the application process early not only enhances the likelihood of securing a spot in the desired program but also presents an opportunity to save on tuition expenses.

Moreover, students can explore scholarship opportunities to alleviate the financial burden of studying abroad. Scholarships cater to diverse students based on academic achievements, financial need, field of study, and other criteria. By proactively researching and applying for scholarships, students can increase their chances of securing financial aid for their education.

Additionally, booking flight tickets well in advance can result in significant savings. Airlines frequently offer discounted fares for early bookings, allowing students to capitalize on lower prices and circumvent last-minute surcharges.

In summary, early planning is key to saving money when studying abroad. By leveraging early enrollment discounts, pursuing scholarships, and booking flights in advance, students can make international education more affordable and accessible. Proactive planning not only fosters financial savings but also facilitates a smoother and more enjoyable study abroad experience.

EMERGING TRENDS AND COURSES SHAPING INTERNATIONAL CAREERS IN THE NEXT FIVE YEARS

The ever-evolving global workforce landscape is experiencing profound changes driven by rapid technological advancements, evolving economic conditions, and shifting industry demands. Thus, staying updated on emerging trends and pursuing relevant courses to advance international career prospects is more crucial than ever. Here are key emerging trends and courses that can pave the way for success in the next five years:

1. Artificial Intelligence and Machine Learning

AI and ML are reshaping industries globally, from healthcare to finance. Enrolling in courses covering AI and ML, including deep learning and natural language processing, will equip individuals with the skills necessary to innovate and drive growth internationally.

2. Data Science and Analytics

Professionals who can derive actionable insights from data are increasingly valuable. Courses in data science and analytics enable individuals to interpret complex datasets and provide valuable recommendations, making them highly sought after on a global scale.

3. Renewable Energy and Sustainability

With the growing emphasis on sustainability, careers in renewable energy and sustainability are set to expand. Courses focusing on renewable energy technologies and environmental policy prepare individuals to contribute to global sustainability efforts.

4. Cybersecurity

As cyber threats become more frequent and sophisticated, cybersecurity is a critical concern globally. Courses in cybersecurity, including ethical hacking and threat intelligence, are essential for professionals seeking international success in this field.

5. Digital Marketing and E-commerce

The digital revolution has transformed how businesses interact with customers. Courses in digital marketing and e-commerce strategies empower individuals to leverage digital platforms effectively, enabling companies to expand their global reach.

6. Global Business Management

Navigating global markets and diverse cultures is essential in today's interconnected world. Courses in international business management and global strategy equip professionals with the skills needed for success on the international stage.

7. Health Informatics

The healthcare industry is embracing digitalization and data-driven decision-making. Courses in health informatics and healthcare analytics enable professionals to contribute to global efforts to improve healthcare delivery.

8. Remote Collaboration and Project Management

Remote work is becoming increasingly prevalent, requiring proficiency in virtual collaboration and project management. Courses in remote collaboration tools and agile methodologies prepare professionals for success in international team environments.

By aligning career goals with these emerging trends and investing in relevant courses, individuals can position themselves for success on the international stage in the coming years. Embracing these opportunities not only enhances skills but also enables meaningful contributions to the global workforce.

THE SIGNIFICANCE OF SETTING CLEAR GOALS AND OBJECTIVES FOR STUDENTS

During the progression from secondary school to higher secondary and eventually graduation, students dedicate considerable time and effort to their studies. Yet, despite this commitment, many find themselves at the end of their academic journey without a clear sense of purpose.

Establishing meaningful goals is crucial as it provides students with direction, motivation, and a sense of purpose in their academic endeavors. Without a clear vision of their objectives, students risk wandering aimlessly through their education.

It's imperative for students to pause and reflect on their reasons for studying, their choice of subjects, and their vision for the future. This reflection not only brings clarity but also facilitates informed decisions about their academic path and future career directions.

Having well-defined goals is essential for making informed decisions about education and career paths. It enables students to align their choices with their aspirations, ensuring they work towards a future that resonates with their ambitions.

Furthermore, students must consider various aspects of their educational journey, including the requirements and affordability of their chosen path. Thorough research ensures that goals are realistic and attainable within their means.

In pursuing their educational objectives, students should prioritize programs that align with their interests and long-term goals, rather than being swayed by external factors such as university rankings.

Setting clear goals is essential for students to maximize their educational journey. By reflecting on motivations and aspirations, students can pave the way for a fulfilling academic and professional life, prioritizing personal goals over external pressures and aligning choices with long-term objectives.

Case of Incomplete Dissertation

Upon returning from his studies abroad, a student began spreading negative sentiments about the experience, claiming it was useless and not beneficial. He discouraged others from pursuing similar courses. Concerned about their significant investment in their child's education overseas, his parents approached me seeking clarification.

I arranged a private meeting with the student and his parents, during which we uncovered an unexpected revelation. Despite completing his exams and coursework, the student had failed to submit his dissertation, resulting in him being awarded a postgraduate diploma instead of a master's degree. Consequently, he was unable to secure post-study visas leading to job offers, let alone land a job. Disheartened, he returned to India and began spreading negative feedback about his experience.

Students should note the importance of diligently following all academic requirements and completing them. Failure to do so not only resulted in the student settling for a diploma instead of a degree but also rendered his education practically worthless despite the substantial investment made.

HOW YOUR PERSONALITY CAN DRIVE YOUR CAREER DECISIONS

Self-driven and forward-thinking individuals possess a remarkable knack for forging their own paths to success, often challenging conventional norms and expectations as they pursue their passions and ambitions. While formal education certainly holds value, there exist numerous instances of extraordinary individuals who have attained immense success without following the traditional academic trajectory.

One such compelling example is Sachin Tendulkar, widely revered as one of the greatest cricketers in history. Tendulkar's boundless passion, unwavering dedication, and innate talent propelled him to the zenith of cricketing achievement despite lacking formal training in the sport. His extraordinary ability to envision triumph on the cricket pitch, combined with self-motivation and steadfast determination, distinguished him as a true celebrity of the game.

In a similar vein, Aamir Khan stands as a prime example of remarkable success achieved without formal education in acting. Khan's visionary storytelling approach and unwavering dedication to his craft have garnered him acclaim both in India and on the international stage. His capacity for self-motivation and determination to push the boundaries of cinematic excellence exemplify the transformative potential of ambition and perseverance.

Expanding our scope beyond sports and entertainment, we encounter trailblazers such as Henry Ford, whose innovative vision revolutionized the automotive industry. Ford's self-driven determination, coupled with his forward-thinking approach to mass production, gave rise to the iconic Ford Motor Company and forever altered the course of transportation history.

In the world of literature, Bahinabai Chaudhari and Sant Gadge Baba stand as remarkable figures who surmounted the obstacles of formal education to leave a lasting impact in their respective domains. Bahinabai Chaudhari, a celebrated Marathi poetess, intricately depicted rural life through her poignant poetry, illustrating the profound influence of self-expression and resilience in adversity. Similarly, Sant Gadge Baba, a revered social reformer and saint, inspired countless individuals through his philanthropic endeavors and spiritual teachings, underscoring the transformative potential of self-motivation and foresight.

These exemplary instances serve as compelling evidence that individuals who possess self-motivation and visionary outlooks can build their paths to success, irrespective of formal educational constraints. By nurturing a strong sense of determination, passion, and a clear vision of their objectives, individuals can transcend barriers and attain greatness on their own terms. As long as one remains steadfast, motivated, and aligned with one's aspirations, there are virtually no limits to what one can achieve in their quest for success and fulfillment.

Choosing the right career path is a pivotal decision that profoundly shapes one's life and achievements. It's not uncommon to witness individuals with remarkable intelligence leading ordinary lives while others with modest academic performances rise to exceptional heights. The secret to a rewarding and successful career lies in recognizing and harmonizing your career choices with your individual personality traits.

Each person possesses a unique personality, and this characteristic significantly influences the most suitable career direction. Individuals can generally be classified into six primary personality types or a blend of two to three traits: Mechanical, Investigative, Social, Conventional, Enterprising, and Artistic.

Every personality type brings forth distinct qualities and strengths, and by introspecting and identifying the traits that resonate most with you, you can effectively carve out your career path. For example, individuals inclined towards mechanical aptitude might thrive in professions such as medical surgery, mechanical engineering, or culinary arts, utilizing their hands-on skills and meticulous attention to detail. Conversely, those with an artistic disposition might find fulfillment in creative fields like design, writing, or performing arts.

To make informed decisions about your career trajectory based on your personality, seeking guidance from career counselors can prove invaluable. These professionals are equipped to offer valuable insights and assessments to help you recognize your strengths, preferences, and potential career avenues aligned with your personality type.

While personality compatibility is a significant factor in career success, it's also essential to consider your intellectual capabilities. Your IQ, or intelligence quotient, plays a crucial role in determining your level of success and satisfaction in your chosen career path. Achieving a balance between your personality traits and intellectual aptitude can lead to a career trajectory that not only capitalizes on your strengths but also fosters your personal growth and contentment.

PROMISING COUNTRIES FOR INTERNATIONAL EDUCATION

When it comes to pursuing education abroad, numerous countries stand out for their exceptional quality of education, rich cultural experiences, and post-graduation prospects. Here are insights into some of the top destinations for international education:

1. United States:

The USA draws a significant number of international students with its prestigious universities, extensive range of academic programs, and abundant opportunities for research and internships. Institutions like Harvard, MIT, and Stanford exemplify the high standard of education available across various fields.

2. United Kingdom:

Renowned for its historic and esteemed universities such as Oxford and Cambridge, the UK offers a multicultural environment and a diverse array of academic programs, making it an appealing choice for international students.

3. Australia:

With its excellent education system and high quality of life, Australia is a popular destination among international students. The country's strong economy and emphasis on research and innovation contribute to its attractiveness for those seeking a well-rounded educational experience.

4. New Zealand:

Famous for its breathtaking natural landscapes and welcoming communities, New Zealand offers universities known for their academic excellence and commitment to research. It provides an enriching educational environment in a unique setting.

5. Ireland:

Emerging as a favored destination for international students, Ireland offers a vibrant cultural experience and a robust academic focus on research. Its universities are highly regarded and provide ample support for students from around the globe.

6. Canada:

Known for its inclusive society, high standard of living, and esteemed academic institutions, Canada is increasingly becoming a top choice for international students. Its emphasis on diversity and equality further enhances its appeal.

7. Europe:

Several European countries, including Germany, France, the Netherlands, and Sweden, offer top-tier education at comparatively lower costs. These countries provide a culturally rich experience along with high-quality academic programs.

Each of these countries offers a distinct set of advantages and opportunities for international students. It's essential for prospective students to thoroughly research the specific programs, admission criteria, and post-graduation prospects offered by each country to determine the best fit for their educational and career aspirations.

COMING BACK AND CREATING JOBS IN HOME COUNTRY

Studying abroad presents students with myriad opportunities to positively impact the development of their home country. Through enrollment in institutions closely aligned with multinational industries, students not only acquire valuable education and practical training but also gain access to hands-on experience crucial for their professional growth. Moreover, many countries permit students to stay back after their post-graduation, affording them the chance to accrue practical experience, secure stable incomes, and accumulate savings.

Upon their return to their home nation, these students bring back not only the knowledge and experience acquired abroad but also the potential to significantly contribute to the local economy. Here's how studying abroad can facilitate students in establishing and managing successful businesses in their homeland:

1. Education Excellence and Skill Enhancement: Studying abroad grants access to top-tier education and training, equipping students with the competencies and knowledge vital for excelling in their chosen fields.

2. Industry Exposure: Strong ties with multinational industries provide students with firsthand experience and exposure to real-world challenges and opportunities within their respective sectors.

3. Leadership Development: The experience of studying abroad often cultivates leadership qualities as students adapt to diverse cultural and professional landscapes.

4. Financial Capital: By securing lucrative incomes and accumulating savings while abroad, students can amass the necessary capital to invest in entrepreneurial ventures upon returning home.

5. Business Concept Generation: Exposure to diverse cultures and business methodologies can ignite innovative business concepts tailored to the specific needs of the student's home country.

By leveraging these acquired competencies and experiences, students can actively contribute to their home country's economic advancement by establishing thriving businesses, generating employment opportunities, and addressing issues related to unemployment. Consequently, they emerge as indispensable assets in propelling local economic progress and prosperity.

OUR STUDENT STORIES

(Note: All names have been changed for confidentiality purposes)

1. Dr. Kaustubh Patil's -Postgraduate program in Health Science in New Zealand and subsequent relocation

Dr. Patil faced initial doubts due to age and family responsibilities but found his path to higher education in New Zealand's healthcare sector through personalized guidance by me. His determination, coupled with my support, enabled him to excel in Health Science. This success not only transformed his career but also his personal life as he settled with his family in New Zealand. Dr. Patil's case highlights the transformative power of education and the importance of professional guidance in achieving one's aspirations.

2. Pratik Mohan's - Bachelor's degree in mechanical engineering from a prestigious university in the UK

Pratik, a bright student with a passion for mechanical engineering, faced adversity when he left school due to a negative experience. Uncertain about his future, he turned to Interedwise for guidance. Recognizing Pratik's potential, I recommended that he pursue a Higher National Diploma (HND) in the UK, providing practical and industry-oriented education. With my guidance, Pratik secured admission to a prestigious UK university. Despite challenges, Pratik excelled academically, gained hands-on experience, and completed his HND. He further enrolled for a bachelor's degree in mechanical engineering, graduating successfully. Equipped with a strong educational background, today, Pratik is a successful mechanical engineer, excelling in his chosen field and making significant contributions to his organization. Pratik's case shows the pivotal role of a counselor in his educational journey, offering support and opportunities that transformed his life and propelled him to a prosperous career.

3. Nikhil Rajput's - Master's in Mechatronics in Lithuania, PG Diploma in Business Enterprises, and subsequent relocation to New Zealand

Nikhil came from a low-income family in India and aspired to study abroad. He assumed it was unattainable due to cost and complexity. But when he came to Interedwise, I was able to help him fulfill his aspiration.

Having a bachelor's degree in mechanical engineering from India, Nikhil sought to enhance his career with a master's degree. I suggested Lithuania for his Master's in Mechatronics, considering lower tuition fees and living costs. With my guidance, Nikhil secured admission to a Lithuanian university, even receiving a scholarship that covered tuition costs. Having completed his academics successfully, he broadened his horizons and expanded his technical expertise.

Nikhil wanted to study further and approached me again. I further curated suitable program and university options that aligned with his budget and aspirations. I recommended Nikhil pursue a PG Diploma in Business Enterprises in New Zealand to complement his technical skills with managerial expertise. Nikhil successfully completed his diploma, gaining insights into management and entrepreneurship.

With the right advice and guidance, Nikhil secured a unique skillset, blending technical knowledge with business acumen, which helped him secure employment in New Zealand and settle there.

4. Kuldeep Singh_ PB Diploma In Business Management in Canada

Kuldeep Singh's journey to pursue higher education in Canada was filled with setbacks until he came to Interedwise and spoke to me. I showed him a way to turn his dreams into reality. Having completed his Bachelor of Management Studies, Kuldeep aspired to pursue a part-time MBA abroad but faced repeated disappointments with various consultants. I recognized Kuldeep's potential and devised a personalized plan for his success, where I evaluated Kuldeep's profile comprehensively, addressing his academic background, work experience, and future goals. I recommended him a Post-Baccalaureate Diploma in Business Management in Canada. With our relentless efforts, Kuldeep secured his study permit and embarked on his educational journey. Kuldeep, with the right guidance, excelled in his studies, completing the program successfully and leveraging his new knowledge and practical skills to secure employment and settle in Canada.

5. Suchit Patel-Post-Baccalaureate Diploma in Business Management and PR in Canada

Suchit, an ambitious man from India, dreamt of a better life and career in Canada. With a strong educational background and experience in banking, he sought guidance from Interedwise. I guided Suchit to enroll in a suitable program and secured a study visa for him. He completed a Post-Baccalaureate Diploma in Business Management, showcasing his determination. Despite setbacks caused by misleading advice from other consultants, Suchit's unwavering commitment, along with my long-term support, led him to obtaining Permanent Residency in Canada. With his PR, he secured a lucrative job and built a successful career, proving that dreams can come true with determination and the right guidance.

6. Dr. Deepti Joshi -MPH in the United Kingdom

A couple of years ago, there was Dr. Deepti, a skilled dentist who had been practicing in India for over five years after completing her BDS. Despite her success, she harbored dreams of settling abroad to further her career and broaden her horizons.

One day, fate brought her in contact with me, a wise mentor who provided her with valuable guidance. I suggested that pursuing an MPH in the UK would be an ideal pathway for Deepti to achieve her dream of working overseas. I explained that opting for an MPH would be more feasible than pursuing an expensive MDS and that she could later complete her masters if she desired.

Following my advice, Dr. Deepti embarked on the journey to the UK. She diligently prepared for and cleared the qualifying exams, including the ORE, and successfully obtained registration as a dentist from the prestigious General Dental Council (GDC) in the UK. With her qualifications in place, she was now able to practice as a dentist in the UK and work towards realizing her aspirations. Dr. Deepti, along with her supportive family, settled in the UK and began working as a professional dentist. She embraced the new opportunities and challenges that came her way, grateful for the guidance that had set her on this fulfilling path towards achieving her goals. And as she continued to thrive in her career in the UK, she remained grateful for the support and wisdom of her mentor, who had been instrumental in making her dreams of working abroad a reality.

Dear reader,

As you reach the final pages of "Wings to Fly," I want to impress upon you the significance of the decision you are about to make. Choosing to pursue education overseas is a pivotal moment in your life, one that can open up numerous opportunities and profoundly shape your future.

Before you take this significant step, I urge you to explore all possibilities available to you. Research thoroughly, consider all aspects of studying abroad, and envision the kind of experiences you desire. This decision is too important to be made hastily.

In addition, I recommend seeking guidance from experienced counselors who can provide you with insights into the current scenario of the destination country. Their expertise and knowledge can prove invaluable in helping you make an informed and confident choice.

Remember, the journey to education abroad is not just about academics; it's about personal growth, cultural immersion, and a transformative experience. Embrace this moment with open arms, and may your wings to fly take you to new heights of success and fulfillment.

Wishing you all the best on your educational endeavors.

Kaamendra Dahat

9798893228601